First edition, August 2011
ISBN: 978-0-9836612-1-4
Printed in the United States on 100% recycled paper.

Cover illustration by Breena Wiederhoeft.
Layout by Zech Bard.

Picket Line is a work of fiction. All names, characters, places, and events are a product of the author's imagination or are used fictitiously. Any resemblance to actual persons, living or dead, is entirely coincidental.

Download the free soundtrack at http://easelainteasy.bandcamp.com.

PICKET LINE

A GRAPHIC NOVEL

Breena Wiederhoeft

for Gladys Wiederhoeft
my grandmother

PART ONE

The summer after college, I moved to Northern California, like so many restless Midwesterners before me.

It was a desperate attempt at a change of scenery, both of the physical and emotional landscapes.

But the mountains wouldn't bring that kind of change, nor would the ocean or towering Redwoods.

No, that kind of scenery change can only be set in motion by a person.

In my case he maybe wasn't a person at all.
He was tall, with short arms and sharp teeth.

PUSH

In California, this type of thing was not so strange.

REDWOODS
QUICK STOP

Pump two.
That'll be $26.
S

TRAIL MIX
TRAIL MIX

Um... can I help you reach that?
Huh?
Oh, ah, yes. That's very kind, thank you.
SNA

TRAIL MIX
TRAIL MIX
TRAIL MIX

Here you go.
TRAIL MIX

Oh thanks! Normally I get the pretzels... I can reach those. But today I just really wanted the trail mix.
RIP!
TRAIL MIX

BEER
MILK
SNACK

Let me pay for your gas to repay you.

What? Oh, no you don't have to do that.

Thank you again for your help.
Really, it was no trouble.

Well, it was nice meeting you. This is my car.

MFB-137

You're from Wisconsin?
Mm hm.

What are you, a cheesehead?

Maybe by this time I was getting a little annoyed by him.

heh

Maybe I was even a little bit frigtened.

Say, what's your name?

I didn't think fast enough to come up with a fake name.
Beatrice.

Nice to meet you, Beatrice.

I'm Rex!

Rex and I didn't become friends that night at the gas station, but he did show me his homemade steering wheel extender.

On his dashboard were mounted two plastic dinosaur figurines.

Makes me feel like a pilot!

That's me and my wife!
He certainly had a sense of humor about himself.

Heh.
Well, I'd better get going.

Well, here.

In case you ever need any lawn care.

So long!

REX HURON'S
Lawn Care
1734 Fern Valley Ave | Finchtown, CA | 95521
phone (707) 555-5616
fax (707) 555-5617
email rhuron@
Rex Huron - Owner

We parted ways...
HOME
GARDEN
STOP

...and it hit me, then,

...how lost I was.

CHAPTER ONE

The first wave of homesickness hit me after a few short days in California.
DAY 1
DAY 2
DAY 3
DAY 4
DAY 5

The feeling crept up on me while I was in an electronics store.
ELECTROLAND
FAST CA$H
OPEN

CAMERAS
As always, among strangers.

It was embarassing to cry in public like that, but I couldn't stop.

HOME THEATER
Sniff

Honey, are you okay?
Yeah, I just, uh...

My dog was just hit by a car.
Killed.
I lied. I don't know why.

Oh, I'm so sorry! That's terrible.

What was his name?
Rex.
It was the first name that came to my mind.

I'm so sorry!

HOME THEATER

HOME THEATER

What am I doing here?

The homesickness persisted...

...but life moved forward.

My savings was running out fast.
DAY 10
I'll have the taco meal.
That's $15
MENU
DAY 11
$60 for gas?
DAY 12
50 degrees... it's supposed to be summer!
$100
DAY 13
Rent is $300 a month.
Ok.
DAY 14
Sigh.
BANK $0
Bill
I needed a job.

SSIFIEDS
WANT ADS

10 years experience required.
Minimum wage graveyard shift.
Don't even bother to apply.
DAY 21
The search was not terribly fruitful.

While paying for the last cup of coffee that I could afford, I came across the business card that I had disregarded soon after receiving it.

That'll be $2.

Thanks.
REX HURON'S
Lawn Care
1734 Fern Valley Ave | Finchtown, CA | 95521
phone (707)
fax (707)
Rex Huron - Owner

On a whim, as a last resort:
Hey, are you hiring here?

Oh, no, sorry. We're not.
ching!

And that settled it.

Beep
boop
beep!

ring

Hello, is Rex Huron available?

Oh, hi Mr. Huron. This is Beatrice, from the gas station a few weeks back.

...yeah, that's right.
The cheesehead.

And so...
TIRES

You can answer the phone today.
REX HURON'S LAWN CARE
yes, we're OPEN
Tomorrow my daughter Liz will be back and she can show you the ropes around the office.
I'd introduce you to my lawn crews but they've already gone out for the day.
Normally I'm out there with them, but my arthritis is acting up today.
Rex took me into his office to fill out the new hire paperwork. Just like his steering wheel, everything was fixed up to accomodate his short arms.
IN
REX HURON

I wondered if he had a specially made push mower as well.

I wondered, how did Rex do this or that?

METER

Good boy!

I started this business five years ago.
SAFETY FIRST
OFFICE

I was a big shot executive living in L.A. but I just wasn't happy.

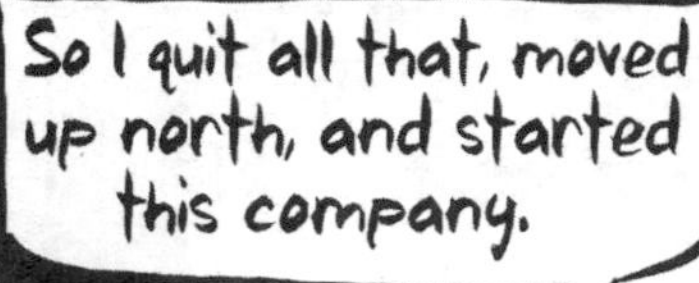
So I quit all that, moved up north, and started this company.

Here I get to be out in nature every day, working with some of the best guys I know.

I never look back.

REX HURON'S
LAWN CARE

We'll get your name printed on there.
Welcome aboard!

Later.
My wife Vivian used to be my partner here, but she's been pursuing other career avenues lately.
hm.

It gets kind of lonely, to tell the truth, with Liz living away from home and Vivian away on business so often.
ah
He talked a lot about his family.

I was spared the entirety of his life story when the lawn crews returned to the shop. Rex took a break for introductions.
Ed
Larry
Glen
Pete
Thomas
They were a gruff bunch, no doubt.

The next day, as Rex predicted, Liz returned.
yes
OP

Clearly upset.

Who are you? Where's my dad?
Oh, I, uh, um, are you...

Um...

Liz!

Sweetheart, where have you been?
Dad...

I swear his arms grew to hug her.

Derek and I are getting a divorce.
CARE

The morning was underscored by the inconsolable crying coming from Rex's office where Liz poured out her heart to her father.

Every so often she became quiet, pausing for breath, and in those moments I could hear Rex's familiar, steady voice offering comfort that was indistinguishable through his closed office door.

It wasn't my business anyway.

It was in the midst of this drama that I fielded my first phone call.

RING!

Rex Huron's Lawn Care. How can I help you?

Hedgeburn Development here. Connect me to Rex Huron please.
Oh, um...

RE
REX HURON
Sob!!
It's ok, honey.

I should have probably known better than to interrupt the Hurons' family crisis with a business phone call...

Um... I'll transfer you.
But what did I know? I was new!

Later.

What's going on in there?

Oh, I don't know... Rex's daughter is in there. She said some-thing about a divorce?

Hmph. If anyone ought to be splitting up it's Rex and HIS wife.
No kiddin'.

Really? The way Rex talks about her it seems like he really loves her.

Oh, I'm sure he does. She can be real lovely.
She can also be a real piece of work.

She cheats on him.
crunch!

So the story goes, anyway.

Later still...
AWN CARE

I think it's about time we got out of here for awhile.

Okay.

I want to show you something.

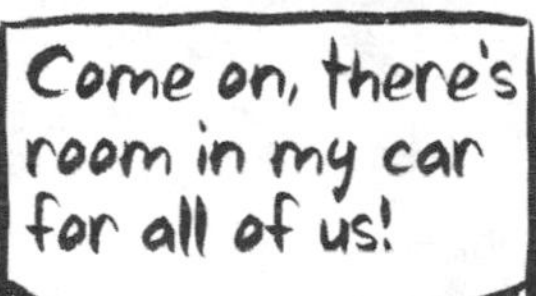
Come on, there's room in my car for all of us!

Oh! Um... don't you want me to stay and answer the phone?
I couldn't imagine they'd want me there in the middle of Liz's drama.

No! I want to show you both!
HURON'S
LAWN CA
Come on!

Buckle up!

now leaving
Finchtown

skreak!

We're here.

NO TRESSPASSING

PRIVATE PROPERTY
of Hedgeburn Development
(Violators will be prosecuted)

This is Hedgeburn's land. What are we doing here?

Oh, but it's not his land. Or it won't for long.

What? What are you talking about?
I'm going to save it.
...Dad, what are you talking about?
You're right, I'm getting ahead of myself.
Hang on while I unlock this gate.
TRES
IVATE
geburg
tswill
Your dad is going to buy this land?
I have no idea.
Alright.
Well?
Where are we?
Mt. Boring, Beatrice.
Many years ago, this was the mighty volcano that formed all of the rolling, fertile land we know today.
Now it's dormant, and more like a prisoner, pent up in the middle of one man's wealth. Most people only ever see it from afar.

Who owns it?

Well, back when California was first settled, a wealthy family called Hedgeburn laid claim to Mount Boring and all this land surrounding it.

Everyone around here hates the Hedgeburns. They always have.

Yes, and in response, the Hedgeburns have buckled and held on to the land even tighter.

A few years ago, the reigning Hedgeburn Titan, a man named Peter Hedgeburn, became sick in his old age.
PETER
hmph

He retreated to his extravagant lodge which is located here on this property.

Yeah, but his "lodge" is like, a total mansion.
I've only seen pictures of course but it's like, these guys are so loaded!

While he was there, he continued to ignore the petitions and pleas from the community to open the land to the public.

But then, for reasons unexplained, when Peter Hedgeburn was on his deathbed he had a change of heart.
Wait...

This is classic!
He declared that, upon his death, he would leave the land to the people.

Cynics would claim it was because of a fight he'd had with his son and heir, Chase Hedgeburn.
CHASE
Hmph.

It's quite possible that's true, although why don't we give him the benefit of the doubt?

Perhaps he'd really been overcome by generosity.
Ha, yeah right.

Whatever his motivation, the community was happy. They believed they would be getting a new state park.
Instead they got a drawn out legal battle that lasted three years and was only recently decided.

In the end, a judge awarded the land to Chase Hedgeburn.
People say he paid the judge off.
Well, that's a rumor.
It's still part of the story!

Chase had long-since declared his intentions to develop the land and put up condos, which of course meant cutting down huge portions of the forest.

Yeah, including tons of old growth - that's what people are really upset about.

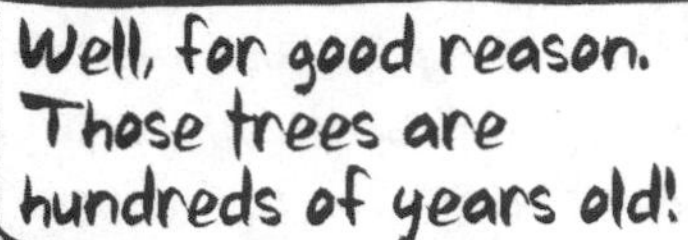
Well, for good reason. Those trees are hundreds of years old!

Moving ahead with his plans, Chase Hedgeburn announced he would open his father's private lodge as a resort to developers and potential investors. A cozy little place to do business.

But Chase Hedgeburn lives in Los Angeles, and he needed someone to be his point person here -

- to take care of the business end of things while he moved ahead with development.
Contract of Development

He offered me the job.

What? Are you kidding?
I'm not kidding.

Well... are you going to take it?
I don't know.

My initial reaction was absolutely not.

But I feel like it could be an opportunity to do some good.

Working closely with him within his company, I might be able to appeal to his decency, you know?

I would like to see him open his land to the public.
I'd like him to reconsider his plans for development.
We all know he doesn't need the money.
So you're thinking about it?
Wow, that's...
...probably not gonna win us many new friends.
No, probably not.
Why not?
Because, even if I was trying to help, I'd be working for Hedgeburn.
And like Liz said, he's not very popular around here.
Yeah, well, rightfully so! He wants to destroy the forest!
I know. It's not right.
That's why I'm going to save it.

Mt. Boring... what a stupid name for a mountain.

You're right, let's rename it.

We'll call it...
Mount Elizabeth!

ELIZABETH I LOVE YOU!

...I love you too, Dad.

On the drive back to town I closed my eyes in the back seat. Rex and Liz continued their conversation from earlier in the day, probably assuming I was asleep.
He has a lot of growing up to do.
Yeah, I know.
And I know you think I'm stupid for ever marrying him.
Of course not, Liz.
Well, I think I was stupid.
You weren't stupid. You were in love.
Yeah, well, there's a stupid way to love and a smart way to love.
You might be on to something there.
Too late.
Dad, do you think he was cheating?
Suddenly I didn't feel right listening in on their conversation.
ACHOO!
It was a fake sneeze.

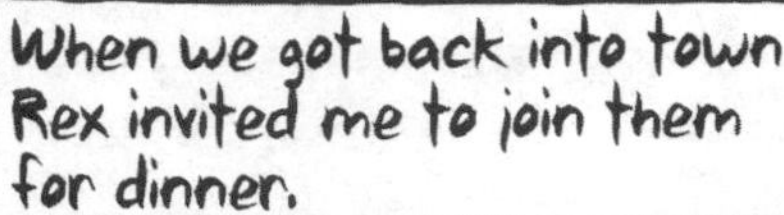
When we got back into town Rex invited me to join them for dinner.
Pity my wife is out of town. She's a much better cook than I.

Do you like tofu, Beatrice?

I hope so, because we're vegetarians.
Vegetarians?

I had trouble justifying this new information with my previously formed conceptions of Rex.
Oh, no need to run– I'm sticking to the salad bar.

So, Mt. Boring really used to be a volcano?

Once a volcano, always a volcano.

It's extinct, though, or dormant, or whatever. It used to be active like 300 years ago or something crazy.

We can thank that volcano for some of the most fertile land on the West Coast.

You might even say it's kept us in business, what with all the mowing jobs we get.

Speaking of which...

How do you feel about cutting grass?

Oh! Um, I mean I've done it before.

Well, you're welcome to work in the office like we discussed.
But truth be told, there's not so much to do that one employee couldn't handle it.

Liz and I were thinking, you might be more engaged working on a lawn crew.
The pay is better too.

Oh, um, sure. I like being outdoors.
I used to mow for my parents.

Well great, then you should feel right at home!

Right at home.

Home. That word was so elusive.

I had a job, and Rex was very kind – but did I belong here?

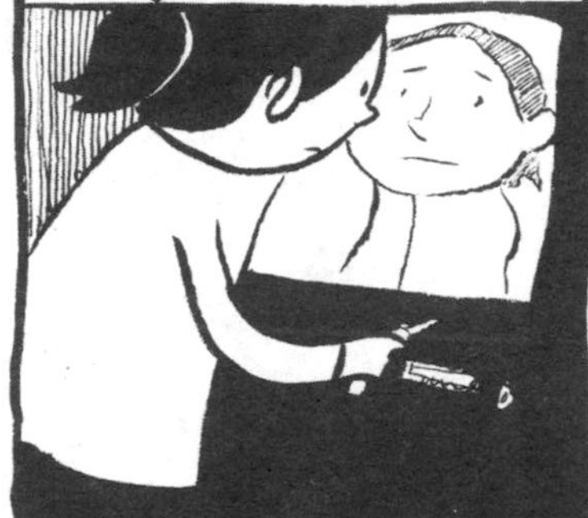

That familiar restless itch – I could run away...

MAP

Historically, that was my solution.

But Rex wanted me to stay. Why? I had no idea.

REX HURON'S
LAWN CARE

But it was enough to keep me there.

CHAPTER TWO

I was renting a room from this lady named Sara that I'd found on the internet.
It was Sara's goal to live a completely sustainable lifestyle, and on Sundays I agreed to help in her garden.
You can put any worms you find in this dish.
Later on we can go fishing!
Nice knowing you, worm.
PLINK
I start my new position tomorrow. I'll be mowing lawns.
Hm? Oh, that's nice.
I signed three petitions today to stop Hedgeburn from putting up his condos.
Three!

That's a lot.

I'd sign a million of them if it would do any good, but I've got a feeling they don't even reach the man's desk.

Maybe.

PLINK

See that plant behind you?

It's Saint John's Wort.

I used to take it for depression.

Have you ever been depressed?
I don't know. Maybe?

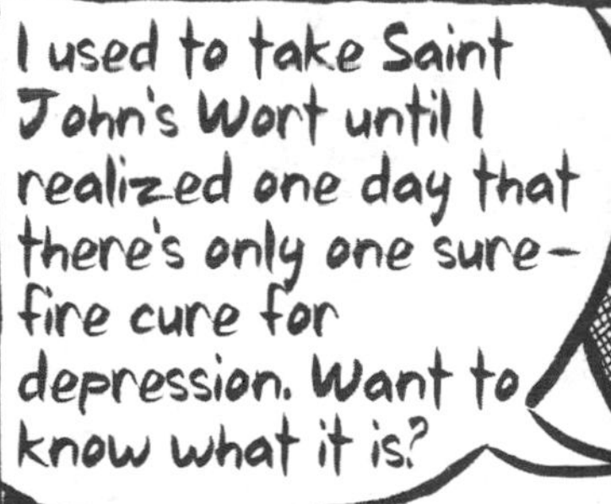
I used to take Saint John's Wort until I realized one day that there's only one sure-fire cure for depression. Want to know what it is?

Yes.

Hand-churned ice cream. Come on, let's go make some!
Life with Sara was a constant kindergarten field trip.

S O M E B A C K S T O R Y

Derek and Liz met in college where they both studied history.
Can I sit here?
Please do.
Met on the bus...
...started a band...
...and got married, in that order.

Liz finished college; Derek never did.

I learned all of this over the weekend from Thomas, whom I bumped into at the grocery store.
And what, the marriage just got rocky?
I guess so? I mean, they fight almost every time I see them together, but they weren't always that way.

I overheard Liz asking Rex if he thought Derek was cheating.

Hard to say. I doubt he was cheating, just so wrapped up in his music and never around.

Rex has offered him a job a million different times but he always turns him down.

What happened to their band?

Derek and Liz's? Oh, that broke up after college when Liz started working.

That's when things got ugly, I guess, cuz Liz felt stuck being the responsible one or something?

Derek plays with a bunch of different bands now. Any chance he gets to play, he takes. Even if it takes him away from Liz for weeks on end.

You know a lot about them.
Oh, you'll see. Working for Rex is like working for family.
BRAN -O- LA
You'll see it all.

BRAN -O- LA
FLAKE
PUFFS
SUGAR SHOCKERS

Why are you getting so much cereal?

It's all I eat.

On Monday morning Rex sent me out with a lawn crew. I would be working with Thomas and Larry at a private residence on the east side.
REX'S

We'll train you on the riding mowers, but for now why don't you use a weed eater along the fences?
Okay...?

chug
putt
sputter

ping
ping
ping
Ow!

Was it too late to ask to stay in the office?

At the end of the day, we loaded our equipment back onto the truck.

Let me help you with that.
Oh, thanks.

Must've eaten your Wheaties this morning.

Ha!

You know how I do.

A couple days on this crew and you'll be juggling those things!
I liked him.

I mean, I was glad I was on his crew.
C'mon, let's go home.

As soon as we returned, I could tell that something had happened.

You're back!

What's going on?
I have news.

I've accepted Hedgeburn's job offer.
Big surprise.
About time!

As we discussed at our staff meeting, he's also agreed to give us the landscaping contract at the lodge.

What, like a storefront?
No. It's completely legitimate.

The lodge will serve as the Northern headquarters of his company, and the property will require a lot of upkeep.

I think it's a solid business decision.

More importantly, it allows me to keep all of you on my payroll.

We'll start tomorrow!

This is the first time Rex Huron Lawn Care will be on the news.

We're going to be on the news?

Oh yes. Like it or not, the job comes with a lot of media attention.

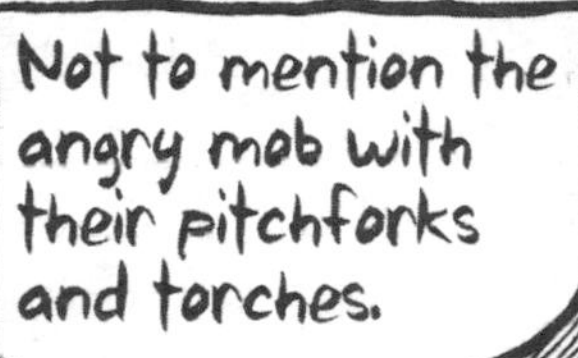
Not to mention the angry mob with their pitchforks and torches.

Liz has been on the phone non-stop since the news broke.

I have a press conference tomorrow, can you believe it?

"I feel like a star quarterback!"
Mr. Huron, do you have time for a few questions?
ROAR!
12
Mr. Huron, a word with you?
Mr. Huron!
Mr. Huron!

Dinner with Sara was strained that night.

So um... what did you do today?

Oh, you know... the usual.

Oh... okay.
Um, pass the bread, please?

Tell me, Beatrice, does your new boss show any remorse over the deal he's entered into with Chase Hedgeburn?

Well, no, he actually seems pretty excited about it.

Hmph.

No, it's not like that. I mean, Rex is a good guy!
He said he's going to buy the forest so no one can cut it down.

Haha!
I highly doubt he could afford it.

Rex owns a lawn mowing company.
That forest is multi-million dollar plot of land.
Not to mention it's been in the Hedgeburn family for generations now.

Well... he said he was going to.

We all say things.

Maybe your boss is just trying to appease his conscience when he knows he just made a very greedy move.

I tried to block them out, but Sara's words had lodged in my head.

They swirled around in my dreams that night. It was the kind of sleep that left me tangled in blankets, not truly rested.
timber

The following morning, I didn't want to get out of bed.

RING
RING
RING!
groannn
RING
RING!!

I definitely didn't want to go to work in the forest.

It appeared I was not the only one who felt that way.

What's going on?

Looks like we've got a picket line.

...what?

CONDOS are CANCER
NO CUTTING HERE

CONDOS ARE CANCER

THIS FOREST BELONGS TO OUR CHILDREN

What do we do?
We'll see.
beep
Yeah, hey Rex.

Rex was following behind with Terry and Glen in another truck.
xssk! Go ahead Larry.
Rex, we've got protesters here.

xxssk! Oh yeah? How many?
I'd say about 15 to 20.
There's 16, I just counted.
Okay, there's 16 of 'em.
And a baby!

xxssk! Alright, just hang tight. We stopped for gas but we'll be there in about ten minutes.

Rex would solve the problem, I was sure of it. He would explain to the protesters that we weren't the enemies.
They would probably even thank us, as they let us pass, for tending so gently to the earth.

Have you talked to them at all?
No.
Ok. Stay in your truck.
Gladly.

This should be a good show.

Hello there.

Go home!
Tree killer!
PROPERTY
WE FIGHT FOR
BECAUSE THEY
FIGHT

My name is Rex Huron. I own a small lawn care company.

We know who you are. You work for Hedgeburn.

Well, technically, yes I do.

I wonder if you could explain why you're blocking this gate.

CONDOS ARE CANCER

You know perfectly well why we're here.

We're protecting our forest!

Peter Hedgeburn willed this land to the people of California. It's not up to some court to take it away.

And we're not about to let Chase Hedgeburn and his land-grabbing cronies pillage this forest for a few bucks!

And that includes you!
Yeah!

Listen guys, I admire your passion. And I agree with you, if you can believe that.

I'm not here to cut down any trees.
You're lying!

Look at me, do I look like a logger to you?

Look at the side of my truck. I'm a lawn guy. I don't have a thing to do with the trees—I cut grass.
REX HURON'S
LAWN CARE
(707) 555-5616

That's still tampering with Mother Nature!

Really? I bend over backwards for Mother Nature if you want to know the truth.

I don't use any weed killers or inorganic fertilizers, and all my mowers are electric.
HAPPY EARTH
ORGANIC PLANT FOOD
HAPPY EARTH
ORGANIC PLANT FOOD

I converted all of my trucks to bio-diesel. Do you know how expensive that was?

I'm just trying to take care of the corner of this planet that's been entrusted to me.

But you work for Chase Hedgeburn. He doesn't give a damn about the earth—how can you say you're taking care of it?

Yes, I'm on Hedgeburn's payroll. So what? Isn't that better than some of the alternatives?
Hedgeburn might want to cut down this forest, but I'm not going to let him.
Oh right. And how are you going to stop him?
I can't answer that right now.
Oh yeah? Then go home!
Well...
Ok.
NO CUTTING HERE!
What's going on?
We'll come back tomorrow.

Are you kidding me? We have a job to do.
I know. We'll come back tomorrow.

Get a spine, man.

So Rex had us work on some of our regular jobs that day.
CYPRUS GLEN SENIOR LIVING

Y'all wanna get a drink after work?
Heck yes.

When we returned to the shop in the after-noon, Liz was still busy on the phone.

Ahh! They won't stop calling!
SLAM!

Who's calling?

The press. Every one of them is, "Can we get a statement?"

No, you can't. That's what the press conference is for, morons.

Oh, that's right! When is that?

In like, half an hour.

Psh. Blow that off. Come get a drink with us.

No, I need to be at this.

RING!
Ahh!

All right. Have fun with your telethon.
Bye.

OL' GUS's
TAVERN
STOP LOGGING!

So Bea, you got a crash course in Northern California hippie culture today!
And she survived!

Ha, they seemed pretty tame. And it's a good cause, isn't it?

Sure, it's a good enough cause. But it's useless in the end.

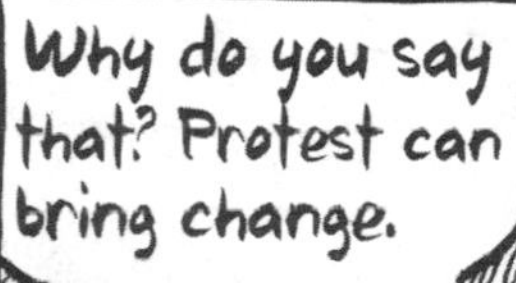
Why do you say that? Protest can bring change.

Yeah. Sure it can.

You're not from around here, Bea. People have been protesting development for decades here but it doesn't do any good.
Fact is, people need houses.

It's hardly a matter of necessity. Everyone from L.A. is moving north. There's money to be made and that's it.
Thomas doesn't place too much stock in the goodness of mankind.
What goodness?
When's the last time you saw anything like goodness around here?
Have you ever?

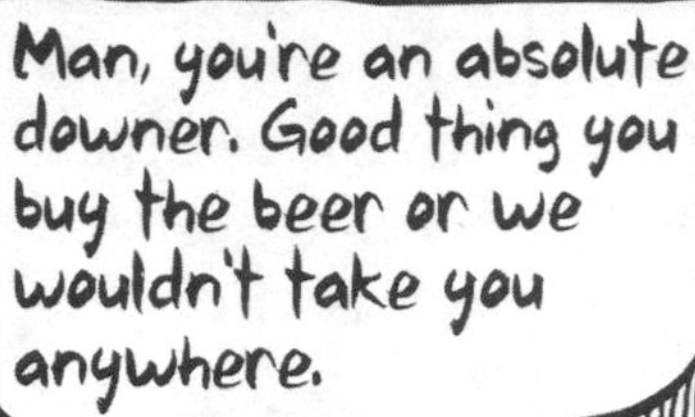
Man, you're an absolute downer. Good thing you buy the beer or we wouldn't take you anywhere.

Well, it's true.

I don't think it's true.
Oh yeah? You disagree?

Well, maybe things are different in Wisconsin...
But here, man, we're a bunch of greedy bastards.

I can't smoke in here. You wanna go outside?
Nah, I'm good.

Well, I'll see you guys at work tomorrow.
Bye.
See ya, man.

Bye Bea.
Save the forest!

Man, don't pay any attention to that guy, Bea.
He's got some kind of big chip on his shoulder.
He can be really nice. And then he just gets so...
Negative?
Yeah.
I wonder why Hedgeburn wanted Rex to have this job, of all people.
Well, he mentioned he used to be in business.
You mean, you haven't heard about Rex?

Well, he'd never say it himself, but-
-he used to be one of the shrewdest, most successful businessmen in the state!

Really?
Yeah. He really had a reputation.

He surprised everyone when he resigned, and surprised them even further when he started this company.

I think it was messing with his conscience-the big corporate life.

Hey, look.

LIVE 6
ROCK STEED Ale

Mr. Huron, what would you say to those who protest your involvement with Chase Hedgeburn?
LIVE 6
Rex Huron-landscaper

I would say, "Let's talk." And we have. And we will continue to do so.
LIVE 6
Rex Huron-landscaper

CHAPTER THREE

After that first encounter, I assumed Rex would be better equipped to deal with the picketers.

I'll talk to them.
That's not going to work.
We have a legal right to cross that line. Let's call the police.

The police? I don't think that's necessary.

All right guys, I'm going to need you to clear this driveway.
HAIK INSTEAD
Hey, man.
It harmed nothing but our pride—
—but the threat of violence turned my insides to ice.
boo!
Yeah, go home!
NOW can we call the police?
No, let's just head back.
It's not a good day for mowing lawns.
HURON'S LAWN CARE

I felt bad for Rex.
He took the attack personally.

Later, I talked with Sara about the protests.
It seems kind of extreme.
People are angry about this.
You're not from here so you don't understand. But people are deeply, emotionally invested in that forest.

But why throw rocks? That's savage behavior.

Is it any more savage than cutting down a tree?

Yeah, I think it is.

You're not from here, Bea. You wouldn't understand.

The next morning Rex decided not to send us to the Hedgeburn property and instead set me up cleaning mowers with Liz.

This will cut through the grease.
Thanks.

So, why did you come to this town?

I mean, it's not the most glamorous place if you're looking for adventure.

Do you know people here or something?

No, but that was the point. I wanted to get away.

What, are you running from your past?

Did you kill someone?

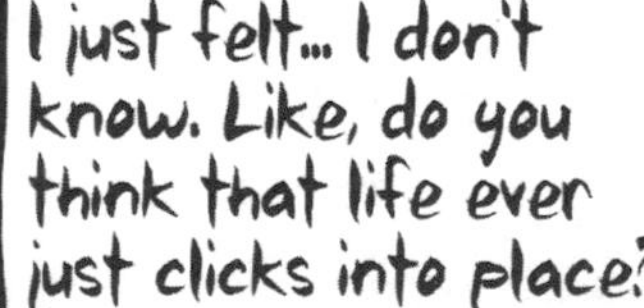
I just felt... I don't know. Like, do you think that life ever just clicks into place?

Are you talking about destiny?
Well, no.

I mean like... do you think there's a point where, if you get to the right place or meet the right people...

... things will just feel right? Like it's where you're supposed to be in life?
That sounds like destiny.

I don't know. But I think I left home because I want things to click like that.
I want to be in the right place.

I don't know either. I don't think life works that way.

I think it's messier than that.

That afternoon I was caught in the middle of another conflict, but this one had nothing to do with the picket line.

OPEN

Liz?

Derek?
What are you doing here?
Liz.

What are you DOING here?

Can we talk? Don't look at me like that–can we just talk?

I told you I don't want to see you.
Come on, I miss you Liz.

Oh, you miss me?

You're on the road with your stupid band for ten months out of the year and you're telling me NOW that you miss me?

I'm here now, okay?!

What do you want?
I want to talk.

I'll give you five minutes. I'd say that about equals the consideration you've given me.
Can we go somewhere private?
No, I'm working. What if someone calls?
Can't that girl answer?
No.
Well, can I sit down?
No, Derek! You shouldn't even be here, so just say what you have to say and then leave!
Fine.
sigh
Listen. I don't want to get divorced.
Oh, no?
We made vows to one another, Liz, and that means something.
I thought so too.

Exactly. We both knew what we were getting into.

"For better or for worse," right? We knew there would be hard times.
Yeah. And we're supposed to face them together. But you're never around!

Don't you hear me? I want to work this out. I'm here now!

You're here now, exactly. Because you've got some-thing to lose.

You're never around, Derek. This isn't a marriage, this is a pit stop for you when you're off touring.

You disappear for days, sometimes weeks, and I'm lucky if I even get a phone call. I have no idea where you are half the time.

It's for my music, Liz. I have to tour – I'm a MUSICIAN!

Oh yeah? A musician or a rockstar, Derek? It takes five minutes to call.

Look, I'm sorry. I'm here, aren't I? I want to work this out.

I don't want to keep having the same argument over and over!

Tell me what you want. Do you want me to quit playing music?
I'll quit.

What do you want from me?
What were they like in happier times?

I want you to leave.

How am I supposed to get over him if he keeps popping up like that?

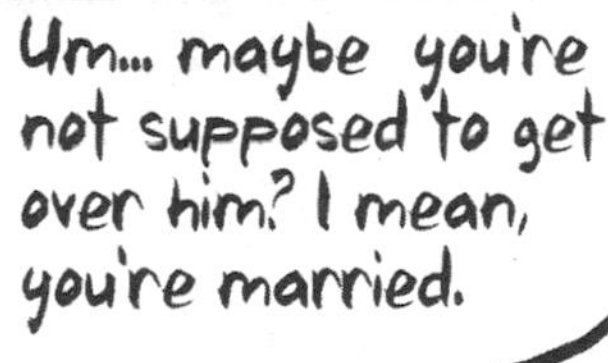
Um... maybe you're not supposed to get over him? I mean, you're married.

You sound like my dad.

I'm sorry. It's none of my business.

But we made vows, Derek and I. That's what you want to say, isn't it?

That's exactly what my dad says.

I dunno. What does your mom say about it?

She doesn't say that much about him, but she's never really approved.
I don't care if he wants to play music, you know? He loves music.

But he loves it more than he loves me. So in my mind, he's already broken his vows.

See? Sometimes life doesn't just "click."

We finished out the week on other jobs. I began to doubt if we would ever return to the Hedgeburn property when Rex announced we were going back.

He offered no explanation and no plan of attack, but when we were on the road we were joined by a squad of police cruisers and I understood: Today we would take the forest by force.

18
POLICE
REX
HURON'S
LAWN CARE

POLIC

CANCER

Mornin' folks.
You don't scare us.

Not trying to scare anyone. Just keeping the peace.

We have the constitutional right to assemble!

You sure do. And these people have the right to go to work without feeling threatened.
So why don't you step aside?

Is Hedgeburn paying you to get rid of us?

I'm a public servant.

Oh, a public servant? Well this is supposed to be public land. So you've got no issue here.

I'll give you ten minutes to gather your things and clear away from this gate.

You don't scare us!
We know our rights!

He would give them ten minutes to gather their things? They opted instead for an uproar.

Their shouts made my seat rattle.

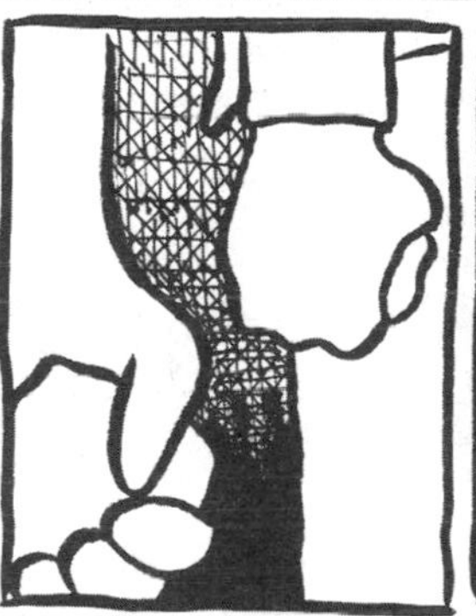

Finally we'll get to work!

Rex should have called the cops days ago.
I don't think Rex was the one who called them.

Alright. Time to clear out, folks.
You're gonna hafta make us.

I was kind of hoping you would say that.

What ensued wasn't quite a riot, but it was close. There was some pushing, lots of shouting, and a spirited flurry of hoisted signs, but in the end, the protesters ceded the space in front of the gate.

What other choice did they have?

We were ushered in by angry shouts and hateful accusations against our decency.

Liz was right– we had not made any new friends.

While we worked that day I could hear the drone of the angry mob on the other side.

Late in the morning, Rex went to the gate in what must have been an attempt at making peace.

Judging by his mood the rest of the day, it wasn't a successful attempt.

Hey Rex.
Mmf.

At the end of the day...

RON'S

I can't believe these guys were here all day! Don't they have jobs?

Protecting the earth, Bea. It IS a full-time job!

Rubbish. These tree huggers are getting paid twelve bucks an hour to stand there.

$12 an hour? That was more than I made!

Interests clashed today at the Hedgeburn property line when local protesters tried to keep developers out of the disputed forest.
Lucy Lamis – reporter

Police met with resistance while escorting local businessman – and recent Hedgeburn affiliate – Rex Huron, onto the property.
Such a shame, what's happening.

We're just looking out for this planet, you know? These trees are a natural wonder.
Sven Holbuck – activist

There is no justifiable reason to cut them down. Not for condos, shopping malls, nothing. It's inexcusable!
But why protest a landscaper?

Rex Huron may not be directly involved with the forestry, but he works for Hedgeburn.

And anyone who supports Hedgeburn must, by association, support his exploitative business.

That's stupid. Rex keeps saying he DOESN'T support Hedgeburn's plans. That's why he's working for him, so he can STOP him.
This guy is an idiot.
Shh.

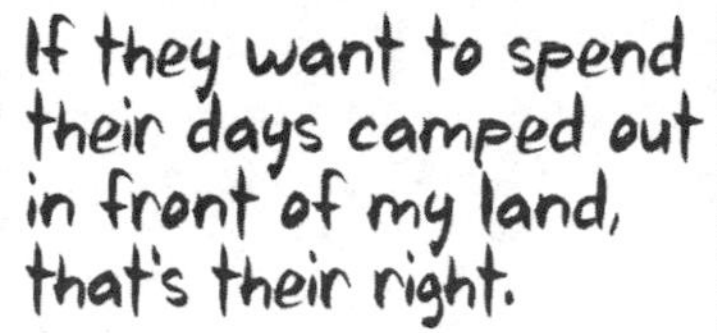
If they want to spend their days camped out in front of my land, that's their right.

Chase Hedgeburn – developer

And it's my right to develop the land that I own.
There are thousands of acres of forest in the state that no one is touching.

And really, where would this country be today if we weren't free to clear the land and put up houses and stores and so forth?

I believe the main concern is over the old growth which is located on your property.
That's absurd.

Trees are a renewable resource. Give it some time, and there will be a whole new batch of old growth!
Boo!

And so developed a hostile pattern which continued throughout the week. The police would lead us through the picket line in the morning, we would work to the sound of their protest, and in the evening, the police would escort us back.

They're starting to do real damage to these trucks. Look at these scratches.
This one is deep.

To be fair, I think the police have only agitated the whole situation.
They weren't doing damage to our trucks before.

They were throwing rocks!

That was an isolated incident, and it was aimed directly at me.

Oh, yes, that's much better.

I don't know what to tell you, Larry.

You wanted the police there, they're there. I've tried talking with them. What else am I supposed to do?

Oy.

You could fight back! Those cops are too soft, but they'll play hardball if you tell them to.

You know Hedgeburn owns the police.

I'm going to act like I didn't just hear you say that.

Hey, if you want to let them trash your vehicles – your entire career – that's your choice!

By the second week, the threat of real violence had escalated.

CRACK!
clunk!

Still, every day Rex would walk down to the fence to try to talk with them.

Meanwhile, the parallel battle wore on, and I was nearly struck by a stray bomb.

COFFEE

Hey!
Hey, don't I know you?

You work for Rex Huron, don't you? You work with my wife Liz?
Yeah, I work with Liz.
OFFEE
Well, how is she? Has she said any-thing about me?
Oh, no, she really hasn't.
COFFEE
I don't see her much though. She's in the office and I'm on a lawn crew.
Oh. Well, listen...
I need to ask you a favor.
COFFEE
The next morning...
Alright, everyone gather around. I need to talk to you about something.
Crap, I'm late!

Well, I've been talking with–
Sorry I'm late!

Here, I have something to give you.
SAFETY SAVES LIVES
What's this?

What is it, Dad?

It's Derek's resume.

He wants a job.

What? Is he crazy? He wants a job here? Now? In the middle of our divorce?

So it would seem.
Well, obviously the answer is no, right?

Honey, look, he's making an effort. Clearly he's doing this for you.

Dad, are you serious?
Bea, how did you get this anyway?

Um, he gave it to me.
What? When?
Yesterday. I bumped into him at Great Bean.
You didn't tell me.
I...

If he gets a job here, I swear I'll quit.

Hey, as much as I love all this early morning drama, didn't you say you have an announcement, Rex?

Yes, right.
Liz, we can talk about this later.

CHECK YOUR
Well, as you all know...
SAFETY SAVES LIVES

We've been encountering some resistence on our way to and from the Hedgeburn property.
To put it lightly!

Yes, well, I've spoken to Chase Hedgeburn about this, and we've come up with a solution.
Arrest the tree huggers?

No, we've decided that, for your protection, anyone working on the Hedgeburn job...

...will live at the lodge.
What??
That's not...
And what if we don't want to stay at the lodge?

Yeah, really. I don't think you can make that decision for us.
This seems like a radical way to handle the situation.
Look, I know this seems a bit extreme but we feel it makes the most sense.

It would only be from Mondays to Fridays, and on the weekends you would go back to your homes.
We think it would be for the best.

It's ridiculous!

I'll give you the weekend to think it over. If you don't want to stay at the lodge you'll be put on our regular jobs here in town.
It's entirely your choice.

I knew right away that I wanted to stay at the lodge.

I thought we were getting along so well!
Oh, totally!

I'll still be here on the weekends. I'll still help you in your garden on Sundays.

You just can't stay in one place, can you?

Heh.
She was right, though.

What was I looking for? Whatever it was, I still hadn't found it.
pat pat

And I couldn't pass up the chance for another new landscape.
click

CHAPTER FOUR

Do you really think they'll tear all this down to put up a subdivision?

Yeah, I do.

It's just a matter of time.

I started thinking about the state of the forest more once we moved into the lodge and were actually living in the middle of it.

I saw the Redwoods as my new neighbors.
My giant, towering neighbors.

The lodge, though in need of serious upkeep, did its best to outshine them.
It was the kind of place that working class folks enter sweepstakes to win vacations to – a real mountain getaway.

I can't say I regretted my choice to stay there.
Where ya goin'?
Man, I just mowed lawn for eight hours.

I'm going to the pool!

Plus, living right at my place of work had its advantages: I could sleep in extra late.

Work starts in fifteen minutes, Bea!

My boss prepared our breakfast...

Who wants some more pancakes?

And there was no commute.

It was also a relief not to deal with the protesters every morning. Eventually Hedgeburn planned to invite investors and other VIPs to stay at the lodge, but until we had worked it into tip-top condition we had the place all to ourselves.

Yes, it was luxurious and it was convenient, but it was also a little strange.

I suddenly had a new group of roommates – all males...

cars, golf, sports...
BELCH

...and aside from the times I showered, slept, or used the bathroom, we spent nearly every waking moment together.

Hearts led,
So that's your trick.
You following, Bea?

This game is too complicated. Can we play Old Maid?

The Hedgeburn crew consisted of myself, Thomas, Terry, and Rex. The rest opted to stay behind, and Liz continued to run things at the office.

Thomas and I were getting along really well and spent a lot of time exploring the forest.

We should catch a rabbit.
To eat?
For a pet!

Terry spent most of his time on the phone with his family.

Marie, you need to help your mom give Scooter a bath. What?
No, you can NOT use car wax on the dog!

And Rex went out of his way to make sure we were all happy.

Okay, who wants to toss the frisbee? Does anyone want a pizza?

Anybody?

Tonight on your home team news report...

Hey look, it's our protesters!
Aw, I was beginning to miss them.

Rex didn't miss them. He continued to visit the picket line every day, right before lunch, like clockwork.

...know you all are tired of waiting...
Whatever he had to say...

...they never listened.
go back to your cushy office lawn guy!
not gonna listen to your lies
...but I think...
Boo!
you must think we're so stupid!
Get lost dino man!

POSTED: private

Thomas, don't you think this is kind of weird?

What's that?

This whole situation. Living at the lodge and all that.

Man, I think it's great. Get me the hell out of civilization please!

And I mean, look at this place!

Yeah.

How do you think Rex is going to save this forest?
He's not.

He said he is.
Be realistic, Bea.

The only way Rex could save this forest is to buy the land from Hedgeburn.

And even IF Hedgeburn was willing to sell it, there's no way Rex could afford it.
He owns a lawn mowing business.

He told me he used to be a business executive before he started this company.

Maybe he has a lot of money saved up from that?
Do you know how much it would actually cost to buy this land?
A fortune.

I mean, we're talking about buying an entire mountain.

Rex is an idealist, and he's got a good heart, but there's nothing he can actually do.

What do you think Rex talks to the protesters about every day?

I don't know.

Geez Louise, Bea, do you think I'm made of answers or something?

Hey, check it out.

Volcano.
You dork.

We had been at the lodge for a week when our pleasant routine was first threatened, by Rex, of all people.

All right, gang. Meet the newest member of our lawn crew.

My son-in-law, Derek Copperman.

Derek was a good worker, as it turned out, and his addition made the rest of our jobs a lot easier.

Do we need to get the south lawn?
No man. Derek already did it!
Quittin' time!

But that's not to say that Derek's presence wasn't, at times, awkward.

Hey, look at that mushroom.

Oh, cool!

I miss my wife.

Who was this guy anyway? Was I supposed to be on his side? Was I supposed to feel sorry for him?

Later.
When I said I wanted a job here this wasn't exactly what I had in mind.

You didn't think you'd be mowing lawns?
Well yeah, I did, but not out here.
Not in the middle of some forest I'm not allowed to leave.

I miss Liz. Don't you miss your wife, Rex?
Of course I do.

I think it's safe to say we all miss our families here.

But we have to do what's best for the ones we love. Even when it's hard.

Well what's best for Liz is for me to be there while we're working through things.

No, it's not.

You're doing a good thing taking this job, Derek. It's showing Liz that you're paying attention to her concerns.
But right now she needs her space.

So you need to wait.

Hey you.

Hey.
Thanks.

Do you miss Wisconsin?

Sometimes, yeah.

Why did you leave?

I'm not sure.

I was feeling lost, I think.

You were lost, so you moved across the country where you didn't know anyone?

I don't know.

You were restless.
I was.
Are you lonely here?
Sometimes.
It's nice having you here.
We make an alright team, huh?
"Don't want to rush this."
WHAT??
I said you don't want to rush this!
BZZzzz
You do a sloppy job and you'll be working overtime to fix it.
It was Friday afternoon, and we were all anxious to return to town.

Well, almost all of us.
Can I please stay here through the weekend?
No. Monday through Friday. That was the deal I made with Hedgeburn.
Bea, help me get it through his skull.
YOU HAVE TO GO HOME!!
I think I'm going to quit.
Excuse me?
I said I'm going to quit. I can't stand being here.
Um, do you think this is a conversation we should have in private?

It doesn't matter. Everyone knows I'm miserable here. I can't be away from her.

Derek, Liz and I have talked about this. She wants you to have this job.

Liz wants me to work for you. Okay, here I am mowing lawns.

But why can't I be working in town like Larry and Glen are?
Because Liz wants you here.

She doesn't want to work with you.

So you're going to have to be patient, Derek, and wait until she wants to see you.

And I think you should stay here this weekend.
WHAT?
Hey!

I used to think the most uncomfortable thing was to watch a grown man cry, but this was worse.

This was a grown man throwing a tantrum.
I can't live without her!
You won't win her back this way.

Liz.

?
I'd call this a double standard.
Not now, Thomas.

We left our trailers, mowers, and equipment and drove back, just the four of us, into town.

It's too quiet here when you're gone.
Maybe you should ask Rex for a job!

Ha! That'll be the day.
BACK PAGE
DAILY FINCH

Look at this.

LOCAL
FINCHTOWN'S HURON DOES HOLLYWOOD
Local actress making waves in Tinseltown with shocking role

Who is that?
DAILY FINCH

That's Rex's wife!

She's an actress?
DAILY FINCH

Rex hasn't told you that?

No. Well, I mean, he said she was working on her career or something like that.
DAILY FINCH

Is she famous?

I guess some would say she's a local celebrity.

She looks familiar.

You've probably seen her on some local ads here...

...It's only been recently that she's been trying her hand at Hollywood.

HOLLYWO
ocal Actress making way
inseltown with sho

Apparently taking on some racier roles.

Oh.
STAGE
DAILY FINCH

I'm surprised Rex hasn't said anything about it.

Monday morning.

What's that?

It's Derek's bass guitar.

That's the last thing he needs, Dad!
I don't see why he can't play it after work hours.

There's not much to do for fun out there.
Are you kidding?

You're in the middle of the Redwoods! He can go hiking, or... bird watching or something!

Don't ask him to give up what he enjoys, Liz.

Did you know that Rex's wife is an actress?

Yeah. I've never seen her act in anything, though.
Rex never talks about that.
I mean, he talks about her all the time, but never her acting.
Maybe he's jealous?
What, that she's getting famous and he's not?
I guess he did seem pretty excited to be on the news, huh?
Well, maybe.
But I meant more like, jealous of the crowds she hangs around with in Hollywood.
The men, in particular.
What, really? You think he's worried about that?
I dunno. I mean, you hear things.
Do you believe that stuff?
Let's load 'em up, guys!
I don't know.

With the fixed blade model, you'll tear through that brush in half the time...

You just gotta watch out extra close for your toes!
Can you hang on?

Hey Rex, wait up!
sigh

What's up Beatrice?
Where are you going?

I was going to talk to the picketers.
Oh.
Do you think I could come?

You're welcome to come, sure. But it tends to be pretty uneventful.

I felt instantly unpopular.

So what do we do now?
Just talk with them.
Talk with them?
Yeah, you know. With your voice.
Hey gang.
Well if it isn't the friend of our enemy.
Come to give us our daily dose of false hope?
Is that what we're calling it now? I've been upgraded from filthy lies?
Oh, they're still filthy lies I'm sure.
I hope you guys believe me that I plan to save this forest.
You keep saying that.
We're working for the same cause.

Kinda hard to believe that while we're here losing our voices for the cause and you're sitting poolside sipping Mai Tais.

It seems backwards right now, I know. But we're making progress. Please be patient with me a bit longer.

Patient!? You've been saying that for two weeks now! They're going to start cutting these trees any day now.

I know you're worried about that. I am too. But I'm telling you, Hedgeburn will not destroy this forest. I won't let him.
You're an arrogant fool!

You're a sell out!
You have no soul!
Yeah!
Traitor!

We've got to get back to work.

We'll see you again tomorrow.
Oh, I'm sure we will!

How can you put up with them every day? They're mean!
They're not so bad.

Sipping Mai Tais by the pool? You don't even drink!
They deserve to be heard. Some days they're even kind of charming.

Later.

Hey, you're playing!

Oh yeah, kind of. I'm trying to write a song for Liz.
Can I hear it?

Oh um... okay. But you have to imagine the rest of the instruments.

Mar

Okay, sweet and then-

-here's where the drums would come in.
Here, you play the drums.

pat!
pat!
pat!

Yeah, and then the guitars will start building, like this - Nee-noo, nee-noo, Weahhh! Wooooah!

I can hear it all in my head.

It sounds great, Derek. What are the words?

Words?
I never write the words!

Mount Boring was really a volcano?
Yeah, I mean, way back in the day.

Don't you think it's kind of scary that we're living on the edge of a volcano?

Ha, yes, so scary...

...almost as scary as that huge glacier that passed through here during the Ice Age!

Very funny.

It's so peaceful out here.
Yeah.
Until they start clearing out the forest, anyway.

Well let's not fool ourselves, I mean, we know that's what's coming.

We weren't hired to keep the grounds of some idyllic little park.

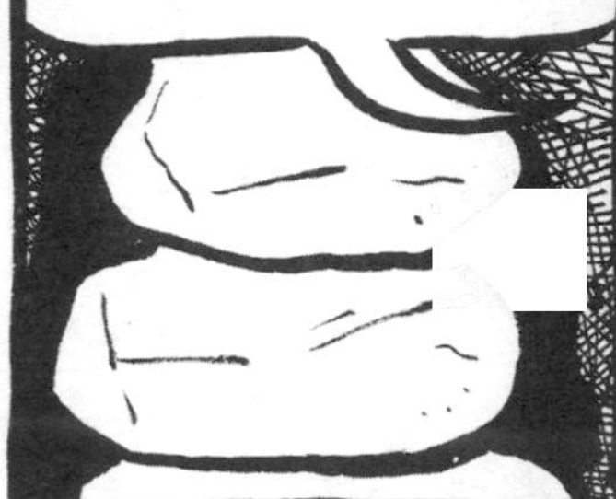
We were hired by a developer, who will cut down the trees, put up condos...

...and pay us to keep the weeds on the other side of the fence when all the rich folks move in.

That's why this is such a big job for Rex, Bea, is because there's so much money in it.

Yeah, but Rex said he wasn't going to let any of that happen.

You're cute when you're hopelessly optimistic.

That's an insult!
I like you.

Obviously, that changed things.

Bea, I need you to mow the south lawn today.
Oh, um...

Can't I help Thomas with the front lawn?
It's a really big job.

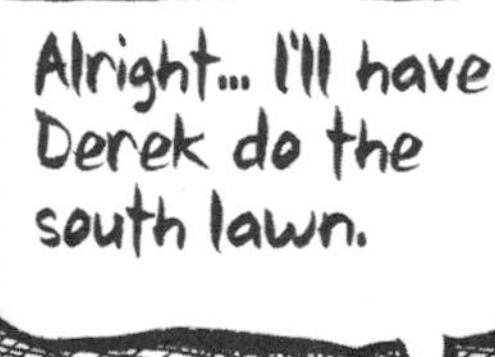
Alright... I'll have Derek do the south lawn.

Later.
Let's trade sandwiches.
They're exactly the same!

Hey guys.

Derek is looking pretty haggard.

He said he's not going to shave his beard or cut his hair until he's back with Liz.

It's like the punk rock version of a hunger strike!

Yeah, well, as long as he bathes. Now come on, let's trade sandwiches.

What, did you spit on yours or something?

No...
I licked it!

Beatrice.

I'm going down to the picket line. Why don't you take a break and join me?
Oh, um, okay.

I notice you and Thomas have gotten pretty close.
Ah, yeah, he's a good friend.

Forgive me for asking, but maybe he's become more than just a friend?
Um...

Let me step back and say this. Thomas is a good guy. He has a good heart. He does.

But how much do you two really know about each other?

...We're getting to know each other.

Beatrice, if I could just not be your boss for a moment... if you don't mind, please hear me out, as a friend...

Be careful with your heart.
What?

You're young. There's no need to rush into anything.
Okay...

It wasn't any of his business.
I have a daughter, Beatrice, and I've seen her heart broken.
Well... I'm not Liz.

I know.
I'm just asking you to be careful.

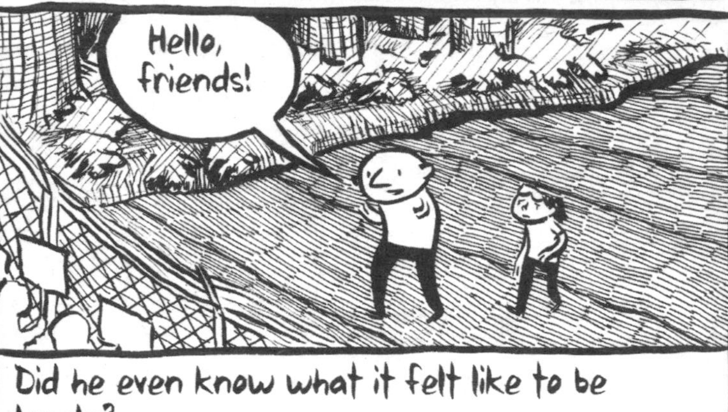
Hello, friends!
Did he even know what it felt like to be lonely?

Later.
I don't think Rex approves of us.
Rex doesn't approve of ME.

What? No, that's not true. Rex told me he thinks that you're a good guy.

Rex thinks of me the same way he thinks of Derek...

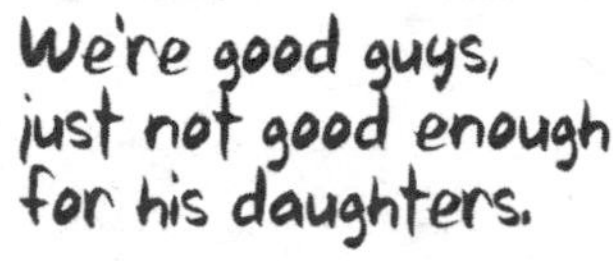
We're good guys, just not good enough for his daughters.

I'm not his daughter.
You might as well be.

Friday afternoon.
Thanks, Bea.

Rex, hey.
Hi Derek.

I really don't want to stay here this weekend.

I think you should, Derek.
I know.

So I wanted to ask you to give Liz this letter from me when you see her.

Of course I'll give it to her, Derek.

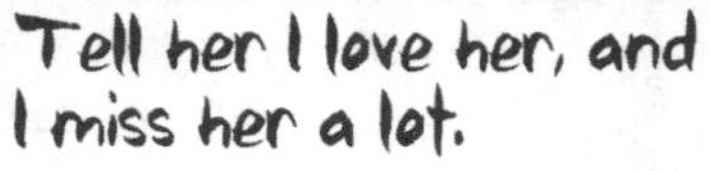
Tell her I love her, and I miss her a lot.

I'll tell her.

Give her a big hug from me, okay? And give her a hundred kisses!
Okay!

And meanwhile, as long as you're stranded here, why don't you turn up that bass a little louder? Make some noise out here!

I mean, who's gonna complain?

CHAPTER FIVE

Things were comfortable for a while, even the work. I was becoming a master weed eater, and as a crew, we fell into a new pattern.

During the week we stayed connected to the outside world – and the situation at our gate – by watching the evening news.

It appears that ongoing protests at the Hedgeburn property line have begun to have an effect.

Since first announcing his plans to develop, protestors have been camped on the edge of his property for nearly a month now.

NO CUTTING HERE
CONDOS ARE CANCER
GO HOME

During this time, three of Hedgeburn's major investors have pulled out, giving the picketers reason to celebrate.

Really?
Whaddya know!

As for me and Thomas, after initially voicing his concern, Rex didn't bring the matter up again.

He seemed distracted in general.

We soon learned why.
I don't want you guys to hear about this from the evening news.

What's going on?
There's news about Mount Boring.

I mean, it's not exactly official...

It hasn't been released to the public yet, although I'm sure that will happen any day now...
Well, out with it then.

There's been some newly released research that suggests that, as volcanos go...

Ours is not exactly dormant.

What??
You're kidding, right?
This man sure loves his announcements.

I'm not making this up. Here's the official memo I received from Hedgeburn.

There had been some unusual seismic activity so Hedgeburn brought in a team of scientists.

Obviously the issue was of particular interest to him, since it's the future site of major residential and commercial development.
How long have you known about this?

Well, due to the circumstances, the research was largely conducted out of public knowledge.

I learned about it unofficially a few days ago, and then officially, only today.

So, what, these scientists just discovered hot lava in the mountain?
Magma.

It's called magma when it's underground.

Ok, whatever, so magma?

Well, I'm sure it's more complicated than that, but essentially, that's it. Add magma to a mountain and you get a volcano.

So as such, the reality is this: Mount Boring could still potentially erupt!

So of course, that changes things.

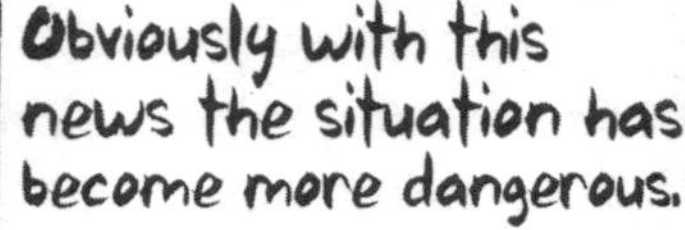
Obviously with this news the situation has become more dangerous.

We'll have an evacuation plan in place in case of an eruption, but if anyone wants to be assigned a job elsewhere, we'll arrange it right away.

That goes for you too, Derek. You're free to work back in town, if you wish.

Liz wants me here.

I'm going to stay here.

In the end, none of us chose to leave the lodge. Maybe we were too comfortable with our routine. Maybe the threat of a pending volcanic eruption seemed too ridiculous to be frightening. At first, Rex's news didn't appear to change anything at all...

...But it would.
I'm just asking you to reconsider.

It's just happening really fast, Chase, that's all. I think it's an extreme move. You're overreacting.

They won't be happy with this... All right... Yeah, we'll wait to hear from you.

beep!

Well, the good news is that Hedgeburn's remaining investors have pulled out of the deal.
Why?

No one wants to build condos on the edge of an active volcano.

Really? That's great!

I bet the picketers are celebrating.
Like I said...

That was the GOOD news.

Rex sounded so uneasy when he said it, and at first I wondered if he wasn't concerned about the business end of it.

What would happen to our landscaping contract if they were no longer going to develop the land?

UNEMPLOYMENT
Will MOW for food

What would happen to his job with Hedgeburn?

If he was no longer on the inside, would he have any chance of changing things?

Guess I'll go find a new forest to demolish.
Nooo!

Once it had started, more changes would come, and quickly.
Beep beep!

The next morning the noise of the protesters was so loud that it woke me.
Yahhh!!
Hiss!!
Roar!!!

Did you hear that?
Yeah, something is up. I'm going to check it out.
Wait for me.

Hey, what's going on?
Why are you guys running around in your pajamas?
Don't you hear that?

Something's happening at the picket line!

NORTHWEST
LUMBER
COMPANY

Rex! What on earth is going on here?

We're cutting down trees!
Chase Hedgeburn, in the flesh.

You can't do that!

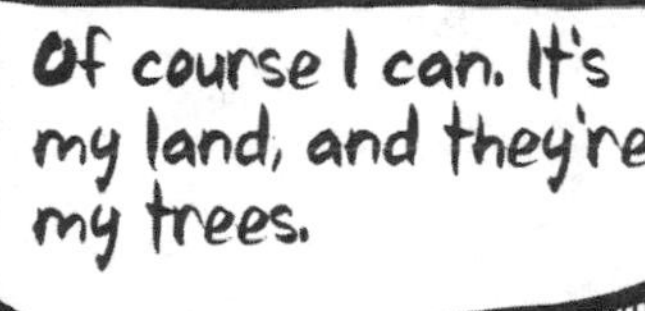
Of course I can. It's my land, and they're my trees.

They'd all be destroyed anyway, when the volcano erupts.
And Lord knows we can't build here anymore.

Rex?

...

It's good business, darlin', that's all.

Rex, I'm heading back, but keep in touch. You seem to have things pretty well under control.

You're all doing some fabulous work here. Keep it up!

And be nice to the loggers!

Rex, is this for real? Why are all these trucks coming in?
He's doing it.
He's selling off the trees.

They're cutting them? You said you weren't going to let that happen!

Hedgeburn hired me to handle his business out here. Well, right now this is his business.

We've still got lawns to mow.

He's right. Let's get ready for work.

Rex! You aren't going to do anything to stop him? You promised!
C'mon Bea.

They wasted no time coming in with their machinery. The roar of their saws was louder than the buzz of our mowers...

ZNGGHZZZN

...and the first time I heard a tree fall, it sounded like the earth had cracked open.

CRASH

Rex was right, there were still lawns to mow, but I had a difficult time focusing on that.

Kerrr-ASH!

I think I need to take the rest of the afternoon off.
Why?

Because, I'm totally demoralized, that's why! And Rex just stands there and does nothing.

Well, there's not really anything he can do, Bea. They're going to cut down this forest.
Don't say that.

Look, I love nature as much as the next guy, but this is just reality. It's about money.

There was never anything anyone could've done to stop this.
You're SO negative.

Forget it. I'm taking the afternoon off.

Later.

Good book?
Huh?

Oh, yeah.

Listen, when I said that I wasn't going to let them cut down the forest, I really meant it. And that hasn't changed.

It sure looks like you're letting it happen.

It's complicated, Beatrice. Every day I learn about a new gray area in life. Nothing is simple.

Hedgeburn bribed that judge.
What?

It's not a rumor, it's true. I've seen the documentation. Heck, I have copies of it!

So you can turn him in!

You have evidence that changes everything! This is great!
Like I said, Beatrice, it's not that simple.

I was shown those documents in confidence. I'm legally and morally obligated to maintain that confidentiality.
So what?

Isn't that why you took the job anyway? So you could change things from the inside?

I was hoping that I could change his mind. Work with Hedgeburn to come up with new policies.

Well obviously that isn't working.

I'm sharing this information with you so you don't lose hope.

Don't you see? Hedgeburn has made a wrong move, and he will be brought to justice.
Only if you use that information!

What are you going to do, Rex?
I don't know yet.

For now, please keep this between us.

Later.
Look at us, walking around the edge of a volcano... we're such thrill seekers!
We'll have warning before it erupts, right?

Here's the thing, Bea. It's not going to erupt.

But Rex said –
Think about it, Bea.

Hedgeburn was banking everything on this new condo development, and it was going perfectly well until the protesters started scaring his investors away.

His little gold mine was starting to fade from reality, so he thinks, "How can I still turn a profit?"

He can't sell the trees for lumber because if the protesters have convinced people not to invest in condos, they're certainly not going to have anything to do with cutting this sacred lumber.

But what if the trees were going to be destroyed anyway? Boom, suddenly there's this "volcano" and Hedgeburn has just the excuse he needs to sell off these trees.

The volcano is a hoax.
That's crazy. There were scientists!

Sure, that HE hired. If you haven't figured it out yet, Hedgeburn's money brings him a lot of control.

Just think about it, Bea, and you'll see it's true.
But Rex said -

Rex is just a pawn, Bea. There's nothing he can do. This forest is doomed.

It sounds like you don't even care.
I care, Bea, I care!

But there's not a thing I can do and there's not a thing Rex can do and there's not a thing YOU can do.

So get over it? Is that what you want to say?

Sure. Get over it. Whatever.

Rex was coming back from his daily heart to heart with the picketers. At this point it seemed like he was only antagonizing them with his continued visits.
They've got some very creative signs today...
So much talent!
Maybe he was losing his mind.

Beatrice, I know that you're upset with me.

You have to turn him in.

It's not that simple. I'm figuring out what to do next, but please, you have to trust my judgement.

As soon as he passed me I knew that I would have to talk to the picketers myself – without Rex present.

I would get the truth. Or at least a fresh perspective on it.

Hey.
Look who's back.

Did Rex forget to tell us something? Did he send you to deliver some more lies?

No, I came here on my own. I wanted to talk to you guys.

I feel like I'm only hearing half the truth.
Oh yeah, like which half?

Well, for instance, my friend was telling me he thinks the volcano is a fake?
That Hedgeburn paid those scientists off?
Your friend is a smart guy.

You think he's right?

Oh, of course. But apparently Mr. Hedgeburn and his big fat wallet are above the law.

What does Rex say to you guys about all of this?

He denies it. Rex is practically Hedgeburn's right hand man. Of course he's going to deny it.

Do you think Rex is a liar? I mean, do you think he really is in this business with Hedgeburn for the money?

He hasn't given us a single reason to believe otherwise. Think about it...

If Rex is here as Chase Hedgeburn's landscaper, why hasn't the contract been nullified now that the volcano is supposedly on the verge of blowing?

Either there IS a volcano, and what you're doing is completely pointless...

...Or the volcano is a HOAX, and what you're doing is a coverup!

Yeah, and your buddy Rex is either a complete idiot, or else he's in on the whole thing.

Everything they were saying could be true. Like they said, Rex wasn't giving us any reason to believe otherwise.

For the next week I lived shrouded in suspicion.

Thomas and I made ammends, more or less.

And as for Rex, I mostly just avoided him.

All the while I was looking out for evidence that would confirm or disprove the accusations the picketers had made.
By the second week of Hedgeburn's most recent invasion of the forest, that evidence presented itself.

Is Rex around?
Oh, um, yeah. He's inside.

...job here won't last much longer...
...you can't afford to turn this down...
What were they talking about?

I couldn't stand the not knowing.
I just came in to get my... thing. I think I left it in here.
Oh, hi Beatrice.

What are you guys talking about in here?
I was just about to leave, actually.

Now you remember who's taking care of you, Rex.

I trust you'll take care of me too!
So long.

Did you find your thing?
Oh... yeah.

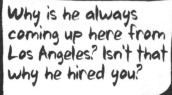

Why is he always coming up here from Los Angeles? Isn't that why he hired you?

Oh, I think he just likes to use his private jet.

So, um... what were you guys talking about?
That's private, Beatrice.

It was just business.
Was it about the judge?
I said it was private.

What, is he paying you to stay quiet?

Beatrice, you are out of line.

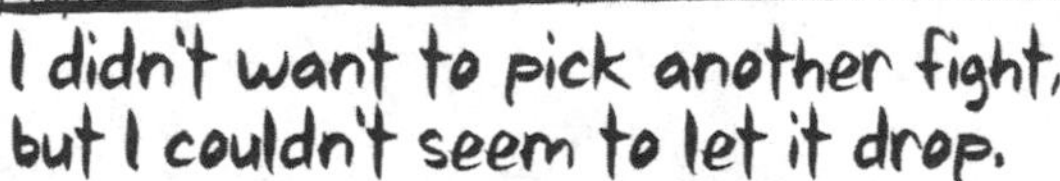
I didn't want to pick another fight, but I couldn't seem to let it drop.

He doesn't even know I have evidence against him. He was not paying me off.
Do you trust me, Beatrice?

That weekend.
What's wrong?
Oh, I don't know.
My boss makes all kinds of promises he can't keep.

Did you really ever believe him?

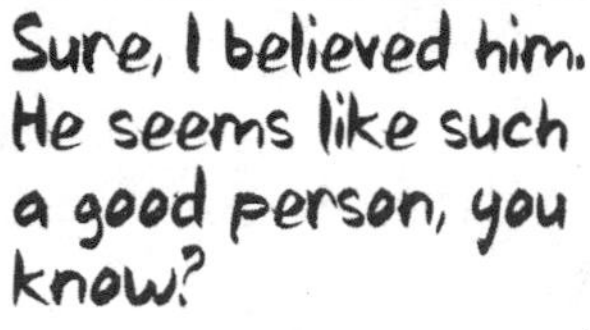
Sure, I believed him. He seems like such a good person, you know?

I really trusted him.
You don't trust him anymore?
I don't know...

I guess not? All I know is that I don't feel right working there anymore. Working for him... for Hedgeburn.

Well... if it doesn't feel right, it's pretty simple what you have to do.

... I have to quit.

Naturally, Thomas was the first person I told.
That's stupid, Bea.
Why is it stupid? I'm standing up for something I believe in.

You believe in a lost cause.
Just because you've given up doesn't mean it's a lost cause!

It's just stupid, Bea, don't quit.
Don't leave.
Don't leave me, okay?
You are the only thing good in my life right now.
Then quit.
Quit this job with me. Help me stand up to Rex.
That won't change a thing, Bea. Come on, I need this job. You don't understand.
What don't I understand?
Rex took a chance on me, okay? When no one else would. I can't quit this job.
What are you talking about? What do you mean Rex took a chance on you?
...
Forget it. Nothing.
Wow, well I can see we have something really honest going on here.

Maybe I don't WANT you to quit with me.
Well GOOD, because I'm not about to!
GOOD.

You can just stay here and be a lawn mower with some mysterious past!

Hippie!

I decided to tell Rex right away and get it over with.

I found him talking with Derek in his music room, attempting to play guitar.

Suddenly I felt very small.

Hey.

Bea, hey, have you heard these songs that Derek's been working on? They're so catchy!

Well, y'know, it will sound better with a full band.
Or if I could play guitar!

Yeah, they sound really great. Hey, um, Rex, I need to talk to you.

Oh, sure. Should we go somewhere more private?
Probably privacy was warranted, but in the few minutes it would take to get there I might have lost my nerve.

So I took a breath and just said it.
I'm quitting.

What?
Woah.

Can we discuss this first?
No, I've made up my mind.

What we're doing here might not be wrong, but I can't watch them cut any more trees.
I didn't tell Rex that I was disappointed in him, that I no longer trusted him.

I think he knew.
You have to do what you think is right.
He didn't try to change my mind.

The trouble is, I can't take you back into town until Friday.

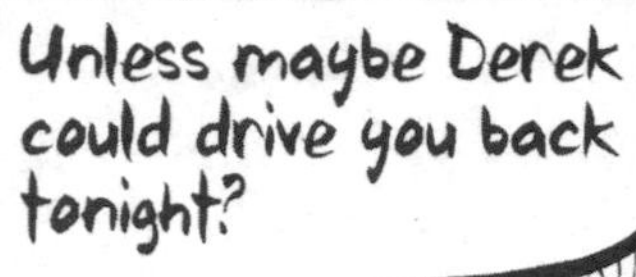
Unless maybe Derek could drive you back tonight?

Uh, sure.

You're sure about this?
Yes.

Well... we'll sure miss you here, Beatrice.

You do really good work.
In that moment I wanted him to say more.

I wanted him to tear up, to hug me, but he was just my boss, and this was just business.

And I had just quit.

I spent the afternoon packing my things.

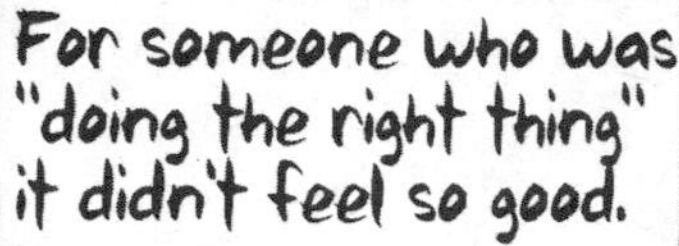
For someone who was "doing the right thing" it didn't feel so good.

Hey.

You're really going to leave?
Yes.

Will I see you on the weekends?
I don't know.

What did you mean when you said Rex took a chance on you?

I don't know, use your imagination.

It doesn't matter, ok? It's in the past.

But you won't tell me about it?

I just don't feel like getting into it.
Okay.

I don't think you'll be seeing me, then.

Goodbye Thomas.
Bye, Bea.
It was a half hug, one arm each, which seemed appropriate, since he only half cared about me.

But it still felt awful to walk away.

Saying goodbye to Rex was no easier.
When you're out looking for a new job, you can always use me as a reference, okay?

And if you ever need anything, don't hesitate to call me!

Goodbye Rex.
Why did he have to be so kind to me?

Derek and I drove out behind an eighteen wheeler hauling a load of freshly felled timber. It was good to be reminded of why I was leaving, or at least why I thought I was.

I understand why you're doing this, Bea.

Sometimes it takes every ounce of my strength to keep from telling Rex that he doesn't have it all figured out.

About my relationship with Liz, about this job, about the forest...
I think you're brave to quit like this.

Brave? Did Derek think I was doing something noble?

This forest wasn't mine, not like it was the people's who lived here, who grew up here.

Was I really so concerned about the trees, or was I upset about the uncertainty?
I had once felt like I belonged on Rex's crew. I didn't feel that way anymore.
The world was so big and I so small, and the search for meaning was overwhelming.
What choice did I have, though, but to keep searching?

PART TWO

CHAPTER SIX

Sara was surprised to see me that evening.
You're back? It's only Monday night!
I quit.
She was delighted.
I think you did the right thing, Bea.
I don't know.
It's always best to go with your gut.
My gut is all over the place.
Well, I'm unemployed.
Oh don't worry about that. You'll find work.
The universe will be eager to reward you.

So once again, I was searching.
WANT ADS
WANT ADS
GLUE

But there were no decent jobs. If Rex hadn't hired me in the first place, I probably would have been unemployed all along.
Sorry.
Resume

I tried to stay busy and earn my keep at home, but mostly I was restless.

And then two weeks in, Sara returned from work, barely able to contain herself.
Bea, I found the perfect job for you.
I can't believe I didn't think of it sooner!

You can join the picket line!

What? Are you joking?
Nope.

There's an environ-mental watchdog group that pays picketers nine dollars an hour.

It's not a lot, I know, but it's something. And it's a good cause.

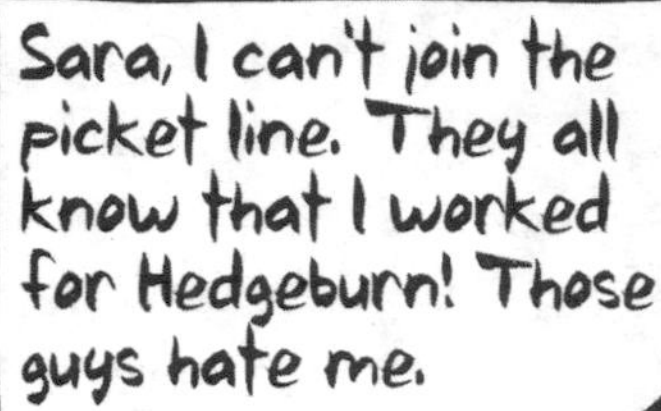
Sara, I can't join the picket line. They all know that I worked for Hedgeburn! Those guys hate me.

They'll respect you for quitting.
They'll see through me. I'm not like them.

Do you want Hedgeburn to cut down the forest?
No.
Then you ARE like them.

I'm thinking I might even join you. Wouldn't this be fun? To protest together?

I can't do it, Sara. Rex goes to the fence every day. He would see me there.

So what? He knows why you quit.

You make everything sound so simple.

It IS simple. You don't even have to interview, just fill out this form and bring it along with you tomorrow.

You can be part of the solution, Bea.
You can do something GOOD.

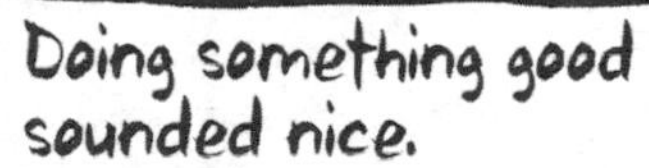
Doing something good sounded nice.

Doing anything sounded better than sitting around looking for a new job. Than figuring out my next step.

Activists needed!
Join the team! Help save the Redwood forest! Enthusiastic and dedicated individuals needed for participation in pro-forest demonstration.
To sign up

Okay, let's do it.

Yay! This is going to be great! I've got some great ideas for our protest signs!

Oh boy.

Oh boy...
ENJOY YOUR LIFE WITHOUT OXYGEN

The picketers met at 6am at the co-op and drove to the forest in a bio diesel school bus.
FRESH! LOCAL! FINCHTOWN CO-OP GROCERY

I noticed the bus before I noticed the crowd gathered around it.
It was hard to miss.

Are you excited?
I don't feel so good.

Um... well, that's one way to put it.
Could they smell me coming, the imposter?

You won't mind if I have to use my sign as a weapon of self defense, will you?
Don't be silly.

This is a very accepting group.
How could she know?

As we got closer I realized that I recognized most of them, which frightened me, as that meant that they would certainly recognize me.

This one had called Rex a tree killer.

This was the guy who had insisted Rex was Hedgeburn's right hand man.

This guy had thrown the rock at our truck.

It was the moment of truth.
Hi. We'd like to join the picket line.

Hey, aren't you the girl who works for the short armed landscaper?

Uh... I used to. But I quit that job.

So, what, are you just here for the money, then?

Cuz we don't do it for the money. It's a STIPEND. Maybe you'd be better off looking for work with the lumber companies or something.

Sheesh, give her a break, man. She's here, isn't she?

Yeah no kidding, lay off, Damien.

Don't pay attention to Damien. He's an eco-bully. AND a hypocrite.
I saw you drove a truck here this morning.
My bike is in the shop.

Ever heard of taking the bus?

Anyway, I'm Helen, the assembly coordinator, and you are BOTH welcome to join us.

We'll leave in about ten minutes. Do you have your forms filled out?

I see you made signs too – that's awesome!

Will you sit with me on the bus?
Ha, of course.

Compared to Damien, the rest of the group was nice.

Hi. I'm Josiah.
Hi.
That's so rad you quit your job!

As we drove, I worried less and less about the picketers and more about who I would see on the other side of the fence.

I thought about Thomas. What would he say if he saw me riding in this big silly bus? He didn't want to join me. Does standing on the opposite sides of a fence make two people enemies?

Love

We arrived, and tumbled out of the bus. That's what it felt like, anyway, tumbling.

So now what do we do?
Well, we protest, I guess.

LIFE
OXY
LUMBER is MURDER
I wished I had made my own sign.

So, the first group of loggers comes through around 7. We give them an earful but there are always cops escorting them so we can't do much to stop them.
OXYGEN

If there's ever any press, though, that's when we really need to make noise.

We want the public to know this is happening. That's our only real prayer of changing anything around here.
ENJOY YOUR LIFE WITHOUT OXYGEN

I mean, we managed to scare the investors away, so you could say we've been effective already!

What do we do when there are no loggers around?
LUMBER IS MURDER

Kill time. Hang out.
I think you're going to like this job.

Within minutes we could hear the rumble of trucks approaching.

Without anyone verbalizing orders, our group morphed into the picket line I'd seen numerous times before.
LAND
SAVE the
LUMBER

Somehow I ended up front and center.
FOREST
LUMBER IS MURDER

Clear the drive!
POLICE

SAVE the FOREST
LUMBER is MURDER
LAND
LUMBER is MURDER
RUMBLE!

CLANG!

That was crazy!
Yup!
We didn't stop them.

Nope. We haven't yet. But we will!

So, what do we do now?
When the next round of trucks come we'll do it again!

Until then, why don't you get acquainted?

Come on, I'll introduce you to a couple of picketing veterans.

Bea, these are my friends Emily and James.
This is like the eighth assembly we've done together, right guys?

Give or take. They all bleed together.
Speak for yourself!

I could give a play by play account of each protest we've been a part of.
Ha, please spare us!

Guys, this is Bea.

She's completely new. She's not even from California.
Hi.

As we talked, I learned that both James and Emily were grad students and picketed on the days they didn't have classes.
Sit by us.
Ok.

So you moved out here all by yourself? No job, no school, nothing?
Yeah.

That's awesome. So how did you end up here with this group?

Really? They didn't recognize me? No wonder they had been so friendly.
Oh, um... I used to work for Hedgeburn, kind of?
I could kiss my new friends goodbye, I was sure.

Oh!
Wow, so you literally crossed over!

Ah yeah, I guess so.

That's great!
Ah, your accent is so cute!

What does your sign say?
Oh, um... my friend made it. It's kind of extreme.

I mean, I probably wouldn't have used these exact words.
LUMBER is MURDER
Ha, classic!
What do yours say?

They're just symbols.
DON'T NEED ANOTHER STRIP MALL

The messages on these signs don't change anyone's minds. The real message is in the people who hold them. The real message is our solidarity with nature.
So poetic, James.

How long have the two of you guys been environmentalists?

Ha, that's such a funny word, Bea. "Environmentalists."

We're a PART of nature, you know? I think it takes a conscious act for people to start disregarding the very environment that they live in.

Oh, I disagree. I think it's very natural for us to live as selfish consumers.

It may not be good, but it's what's the easiest. And humans love easy.

Well either way, we've been working for environmental causes for four years now.
What about you?

Oh, hm... I started fighting for the environment about... two hours ago?
Ha!

Really, I don't think I belong here.
Why do you say that?

It's just that I never thought twice about the environment before I was thrown in the middle of all this.

I think this forest and mountains are beautiful...
I couldn't be part of cutting them down...
...but...

We do need wood, right? I mean, we need lumber to build houses and schools and churches and stuff, right?

Oh, of course. This isn't about protesting the lumber industry. At least that's not why Emily and I are here.

But this particular forest is hundreds of years old! That's an incredibly important part of history. More important than another subdivision!

Think of it like... like when people protest the demolition of a historical building.

There are lots of other places to build, and lots of other places to get lumber.
Yeah, so trust us, Bea.

You belong here. I mean, no less than the rest of us.

While talking with James and Emily I almost forgot about the inevitable fence-visit from Rex.

I imagined I could hear him approaching before I saw him.

But of course, it was nothing like that.
Hey, here comes Rex.
Yay!

Wait, you guys LIKE Rex? But he works for Hedgeburn.

He's a nice guy. And he pays attention to us.
Don't worry, we still give him hell. That's our job.

Rex's good reputation with the protesters made little difference to me.

The fact remained that I had defected from his ranks and joined the other side. I had chewed up his kindness. Seeing me here would be like spitting it back in his face.
You coming Bea?

At first I couldn't see him at all.

But when the noise of the protest lowered, there was his familiar voice, the familiar false promises.
I DON'T THINK YOU'LL NEED TO STAY HERE MUCH LONGER. I THINK WE'RE GOING TO SEE SOME POLICY CHANGES REAL SOON...

It reminded me why I had quit working for him, and I was filled with sudden indignation.
INSTEAD

LUMBER is MURDER

Beatrice?

My anger melted when I saw his face.

Hi Rex.
LUMBER is

You joined the picket line?
Yeah... I'm sorry.

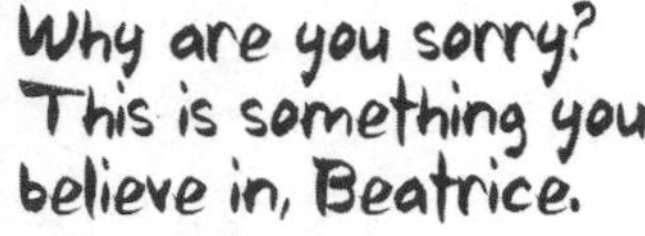
Why are you sorry? This is something you believe in, Beatrice.

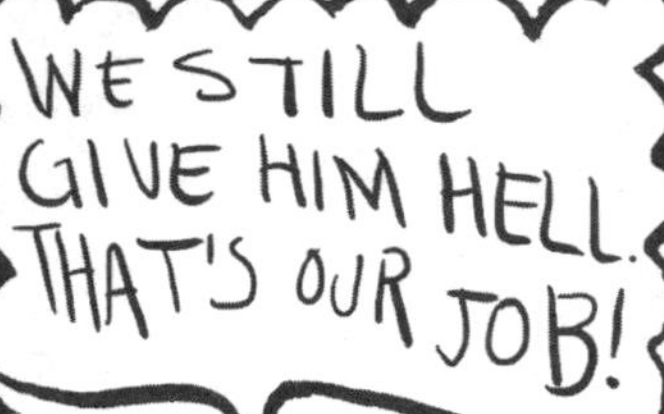
WE STILL GIVE HIM HELL. THAT'S OUR JOB!

You've got to end this, Rex.

You've got to do what you promised or cut your ties with Hedgeburn.
Yeah!
Totally!

Bea, I'll ask the same thing of you that I ask all the rest. Please be patient.

Be patient? But you've been saying that for –

You're all talk, man!

Down with Hedgeburn!
Yeah!
FOREST

Once again, their shouts were drowning him out.

NO SOUL!
HAVE BEEN
QUIT LYING TO US, MAN
GO BACK TO YOUR CAVE!
You're just a Sell OUT!

And I was sucked back into the picket line.

HAIR INSTEAD

What was he saying to you?

I couldn't tell.

Oh well, it was probably a bunch of hot air anyway, you know?

I mean, he's a nice guy and all, but he uses the same lines over and over again.

Yeah.

Hey let's grab James and go eat lunch.

Maybe Rex wasn't that good of a guy.

Sure, he ran what seemed to be an honest business, took good care of his employees and family. He never cursed and never cheated... could he be a liar?

He said he had a plan, but did I have any reason to trust him? The only bit of leverage that he had, he refused to employ, if it was any leverage at all.

If he did have a plan, he was taking his dangerously sweet time. Every day the lumber trucks came and went with another slice of the forest to put up for sale.

Later that week I remembered that I had told Derek I would visit Liz. Sara and I came home early one afternoon, and even though part of me was scared to show up at the office after all that had happened, I wanted to keep my word.

REX HURON'S
LAWNCARE

Hi Liz.
Well well, if it isn't the defector herself.

Did you come to ask for your job back?

Oh um... no. I just came to say hi, actually.

You walk out on my family's business and you think you can just stroll back in to say hi?

Woah, Liz, it was nothing personal! I just felt that –

You're laughing.

I'm just messing with you.

We think it's awesome that you quit. Not like, oh good she's gone, but you know, ballsy.

Oh, cool. Who is "we"?

Derek and me.

Oh... you guys are in touch now?

Oh, he writes me letters

You know, I think even my dad respects you for quitting.
Yeah right.

Who am I? Just some weird girl who begged for a job and then stormed off a few months later.

He probably thinks I'm unbalanced.
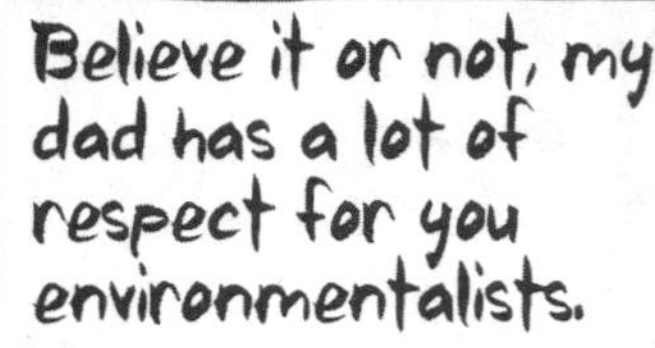
Believe it or not, my dad has a lot of respect for you environmentalists.

Oh gosh, I'm hardly an environmentalist.
You joined the picket line!

And I mean, you quit to like, save the trees, didn't you?
Is that why I quit?

Liz, your dad said he was going to save the forest.

Yeah, I recall that conversation.

Well... was he lying?
My dad doesn't lie.

So you think he'll do it?
I think he'll sure try.

So Derek thought you and I could hang out sometime, now that I'm back in town.

That would be fun. I mean, if you're not too busy hugging trees, and all.
Hilarious.

I thought so. Come on, let's get lunch.
Ya hippie.

Do you want to know what makes my dad a good person?
Yes, I'd like to hear that.
CIRCL
'ROUN
CAFE
OPEN

I'll give you three simple reasons. He's completely selfless, he's completely loyal, and he wants to do what's right.

That's not common, you know. That's not ordinary.

No, I guess it's not.

But my dad is an idealist. That's his flaw. His faith in mankind tends to go beyond humanity's actual potential for goodness.

It gets him into trouble sometimes.

What about your mom?
Ha, well, she's another story.

She can be such a good person. And then sometimes she just completely disappoints.

I heard that she's an actress?

Yeah, she's trying to be! She's gone a lot because of it.

I mean, she comes and goes. You should meet her, though, the next time she's back at home.
Ok.

I can't believe you joined the picketers. You really are all over the board!

Oh, trust me...
I'm well aware.

CHAPTER SEVEN

With every day that passed, the number of loggers coming and going seemed to grow. If there had been an underlying sense of urgency before, now it was right there in our faces.

Hedgeburn seemed desperate to squeeze every last penny from his resources, and made quite a show about the "race against the natural clock." His theatrics rivaled his cutthroat business practices.

I caught a glimpse of Thomas working on a few occasions, but he never came near the fence.

I missed him a lot, but for some reason, he still represented something ugly to me.

Over the weekend, Liz invited me to dinner.

Mom is getting in to town tonight. You could meet her.

Um, sure I guess.

You'll come? Great! Dad said he'd like to see you anyway.

Rex is going to be there?

Well duh, she's his wife.

chirp!

Sara was very interested when I mentioned Rex's wife was going to be in town.

She's back?

Yeah.

I really didn't think we would be seeing her around town anymore.

Why wouldn't she come back? They're married.

Oh, well I hate to be a gossip, but it's just about common knowledge that their marriage is on the rocks these days.

Some people say she's taken up with the director of that movie she's shooting.

What do you mean, taken up with?

You know. That they're sleeping together. I think she stays at his house when she's down there.

And then there are the rumors that she's been getting friendly with Hedgeburn himself.

Two lonely souls just trying to get by in Los Angeles, I guess.

What? Does Rex know about that?

He must, he's not stupid. Everyone in town knows about it.

The last time she left everyone thought it would be for good.
Ptoo!

Neither Rex nor Liz had so much as hinted that anything was amiss.

But then, I guess they wouldn't. I guess it was probably not something they liked to talk about.
I'd pay good money to watch the drama tonight.

Take notes, I'll want a play by play!

That night I was nervous. Would Rex even welcome me into his home?

Hello Beatrice.
Hi Rex.

It's good to see you again without a chain link fence between us.
Is she here?

Yes dear.
Bea, I'd like you to meet my wife, Vivian.

I'd seen a grainy photo in the paper, and others framed in Rex's office, but she looked familiar for another reason...
Hi dear.

We're so glad you could join us, Bea. Rex and Liz have told me so much about you.

And something about the way she smiled so warmly jogged my memory.

Did she recognize me? She had seen me sobbing in the digital camera aisle. I had named my fictional dog after her husband!

You just make yourself at home, Bea.
Can I get you something to drink?
If she did recognize me, she never mentioned it.

Later.
After my audition I was expecting to get a bit role, if anything.
I mean, I would have gladly taken the part of a janitor in the background!

You're too talented for bit roles.

Psh. Well, there's a pecking order you just don't want to disturb, you know?

And so, when they offered me the role of Darlene I was a bit frightened, actually!

I worried I may have offended some of the more seasoned actresses auditioning.

Haha, oh yeah, I can just imagine you getting into a cat fight with some big Hollywood Divas, mom.

I was so nervous, really! But somehow I caught the director's eye, and it's been an absolute whirlwind ever since!

Wouldn't it be nice if that whirlwind brought you home a little more often?

Oh Rex, please. You know there aren't any opportunities for actors up here.

Rex can be so silly.
Did you know he used to be the Vice President of Henning Tech?

I don't know what that is.

It's a Fortune 500 fiber optics company.

They were even talking about making him president when Rex got his ridiculous idea to start his little lawn mowing company.
And I've never regretted it.

We lived in this fantastic little ranch home in Beverly Hills.

I was traveling overseas every other week.

I just think it was such a silly idea to move up here, with all that Los Angeles has to offer. I've been praying for a chance to get him back into business.

I mean, REAL business, none of this inane manual labor.

Looks like you might get that chance.
Vivian.

What? Well can I tell them? No, you're right, you should tell them.

COUGH

I'll tell them.

Rex was offered a job!
What? Which job?

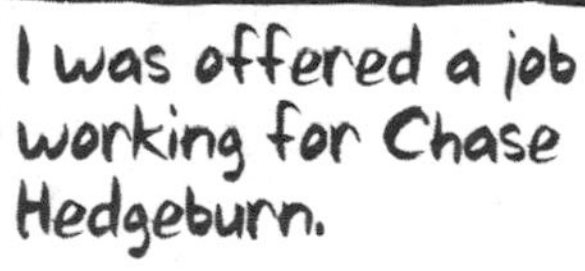
I was offered a job working for Chase Hedgeburn.

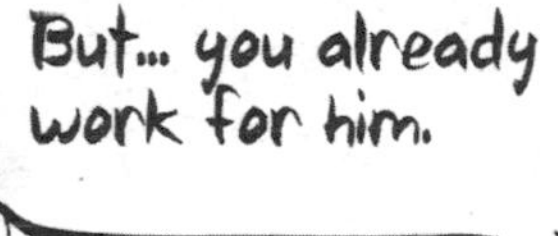
But... you already work for him.

As a contractor. This would be a promotion, Chase wants to make Rex a full partner, can you believe it?

It's true. Chase has been keen to point out that the job at the lodge won't last much longer. He's only keeping the lawn care contract in place as a favor to me.

That's how he's presenting it, anyway. He's offering me a job in Los Angeles, managing some of his top accounts.

Isn't that wonderful?

I haven't accepted.
But he hasn't declined.

Can you imagine? The whole family back in Los Angeles. Liz, you could come too, get a fresh start.

KNOCK KNOCK

Who could that be?

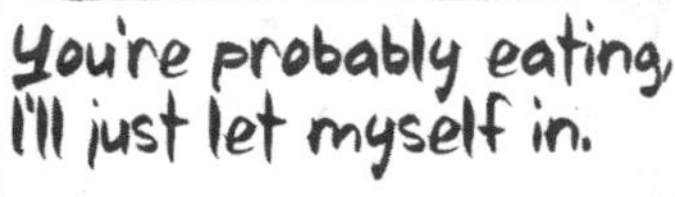
You're probably eating, I'll just let myself in.

Hi.

Derek...

It's okay, Dad. I asked him to come.

These are for you.

Hello Derek. How nice of you to join us.
I asked him to come, mom.

I hear you're working for Rex these days.

Yes ma'am. Making a real live paycheck.

He's real good at what he does.
That's funny...

I thought what he does is run around being a rock star.
Mom...

You know, leaving my daughter behind and all.
Vivian.

With all due respect, Vivian, when's the last time you came home before tonight?

Derek!

No, that's fair.

Good boy, that's more than fair.
I'll get dessert.

If Sara had paid good money for some drama, she might have been disappointed. To my relief, the tension at the dinner table never reached a head.

Dad said he and Mom will clean up.

Do you guys want to watch a movie?
Sure.
Ok.

Sorry Mom was kind of cold to you.
's okay.

I think once she sees you're not doing the band thing anymore she'll ease up, y'know?

You're a working man now!
Right.

This is Derek's favorite movie.

You shaved your beard off.
Yeah, for Liz.

What? You had a beard? I wish I could have seen that!
"vegas, baby, vegas!"

They started kissing about ten minutes into the movie, at which point I excused myself.
"I'll have the pancakes in the age of enlightenment."
See ya.

Hey Rex.

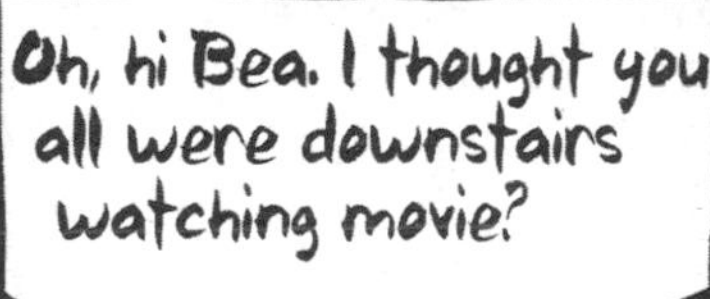
Oh, hi Bea. I thought you all were downstairs watching movie?

Yeah, I'm just taking a break. Where's Vivian?
Vivian went for a walk.

She... needed some fresh air.
Oh. What are you reading?

Aldo Leopold. The Sand County Almanac.
Oh.
How's Thomas?

Thomas is...
Thomas is... doing okay.

He misses you a lot, but then we all do.

Are you mad that I joined the picket line?
I'm not.

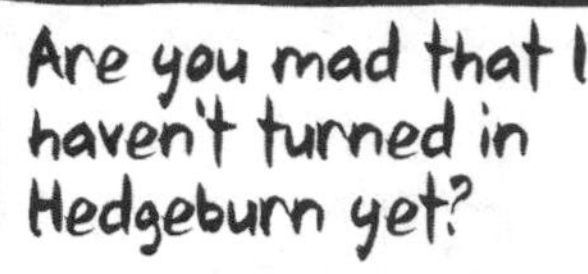
Are you mad that I haven't turned in Hedgeburn yet?

A little, yes.

When you caught the tail end of that conversation back at the lodge, he wasn't trying to bribe me, I can assure you of that, Bea.

Then what was he talking about?

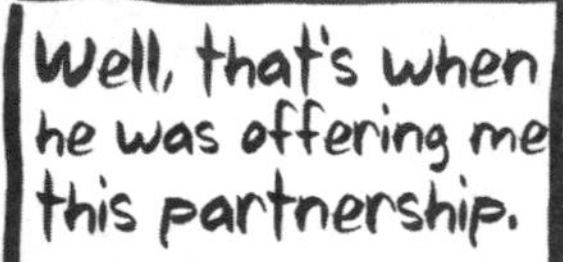
Well, that's when he was offering me this partnership.

Oh, right.

A real job, as Vivian would say.
Are you going to take it?

I won't lie, the offer is very tempting. The pay is good, the work would be challenging...

And it would mean Vivian wouldn't have to be away as much, since I would be down there with her.

She's angry with me. She can't understand why I would even hesitate.

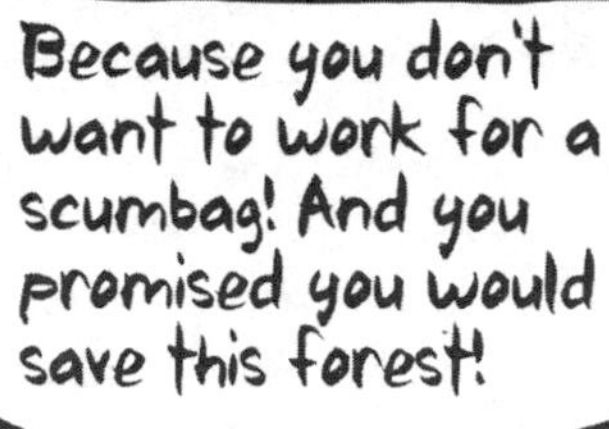
Because you don't want to work for a scumbag! And you promised you would save this forest!

I know.

So what are you going to do?
... I want Vivian to be happy.

Want to hear some-thing strange? I met your wife once before.
Really?

I don't think she recognized me tonight but I met her one of my first days in town.

I was homesick, and crying like a baby, and she gave me a hug.
Well what do y'know!

I mean, that's Viv for you. She can be really quite loving sometimes.

What are you going to do?
... I don't know.

The next morning.
You guys want some oatmeal?
Sure, I'm starving.
Here come the police.

LUMBER IS MURDER
Admittedly it was an unusual day job.

Later.
Hello picketers.

You good for nothing capitalist!
...you good for...nothing...
CONDOS ARE
NCER
I had just eaten dinner with this man. We had talked candidly in his living room.

Had I not yet picked a side?

The notion of the volcano became widely known as a joke among the picketers, and even Rex seemed hesitant to admit its existence.

Is it getting hot over there on top of all that lava?

Oh yes, it's a regular Pompeii over here, heh.

But then, one day, there was an eruption.

It was a small one, it sounded like a faint grumble in the distance, and although I didn't see it when it happened, the smoke cloud stayed over the mountain for the rest of the day.

The eruption made the evening news, as did Hedgeburn, who acted like he had just been vindicated.
Of course we knew it was only a matter of time.

Naturally, this only heightens the need to harvest the trees before the next, more devastating eruption.

I wondered if this mildly catastrophic event would cause the picketers to opt out, to retreat en masse to safer grounds.
There's no need to leave.
As long as Hedgeburn has his men in there it's got to be safe.

If there was a real threat he would have pulled everyone out by now.

A lot of people are saying it was a hoax, anyway.
NEED

We don't usually get caught up in conspiracy theories...
But it IS a little suspicious how the timing is working out.
NEED

In the days following the eruption, Rex didn't stay at the fence long, and I didn't get to talk with him.
Did you guys hear the latest about this "volcano?"
Apparently Hedgeburn paid some one on the inside to fake that eruption!
Yeah, well...
Who really ever believed it was going to erupt?
That guy is getting so desperate!
I missed Thomas.
At lunchtime I took a walk along the fence line.

WHIRRRRRRRRRR

RRRRR

RRRR

Bea?

What are you doing here?
Working.
Oh yeah, I heard about that.

You knew I was on the picket line?
Yeah.

You never came by to see me.

You made it pretty clear you didn't want to see me.
Oh, right...

I don't know why I said that... I miss you.

I miss you too.

So... you really ARE a hippie now!
Oh, please.

And I see Rex has demoted you to weed eater.
Psh. I dominate this thing.

Man. I can't believe you've been gone for, what, like, three weeks now?

It feels like it's been longer.

Are you happy you left?

Yeah, I think so. Are you happy you stayed?

Haha...

Have I ever been happy?

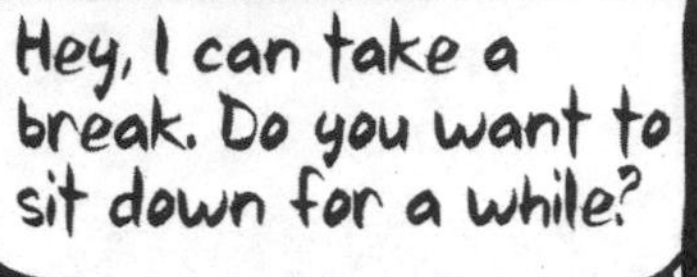
Hey, I can take a break. Do you want to sit down for a while?

Sure.

We sat as close as we could, with the fence dividing us, our unflapable chaperone.
It is so nice to see you.
You too, Bea, really.

So what are you going to do when all this is over? Find another picket line?
I don't know.

I mean, eventually I do want to settle into something, somewhere.

Once you find "your place" in the world?

Yeah.

Do you think I'll ever find mine?

I didn't know you were looking.
Well...

...maybe I should start.

You could still join the picket line. It's not too late.

You know, I'd almost consider joining it, just to be around you again.

You've still told me almost nothing about yourself.

I keep hoping you'll lose interest in that.

In your life?

Hey, if you're looking for purpose, Bea, I don't think you're going to find it in me.

The forest might still have a hope in heaven. Me? I'm beyond saving.
Thomas, don't say—

ROAR!

ROAR!

What's going on?
Hang on.

NOT YOUR LAND
THIS FOREST BELONGS TO
Reporters.

James!
Bea, check it out–reporters from every station!

Time to get loud!
What are they here for?
They hadn't made a single appearance since I'd joined the picket line.

I'm not totally sure. I think Hedgeburn is getting busted for faking that eruption the other day?

Emily went to get the details and now they want to interview her.

It's all kind of a big confused mess, but one thing we know – when the media comes, we get loud!

I'm gonna talk to Emily.

What's going on, Em?
I'm going to be on TV!
Remember, look here, not at the camera.
NOT YOUR LAND
We're rolling!

Reports began circulating today that the recent eruption of Mount Boring was manufactured and that Hedgeburn Development may have been at the helm.

How do you react, miss, considering your long-standing opposition to the logging and to Hedgeburn's business policies in general?

If those things are true, we're certainly glad they've been brought to light.
LIVE

I mean, we could give you a hundred other reasons why lumber companies shouldn't do business with Chase Hedgeburn...

For instance...
Yeah ok.
How 'bout another riveting interview?

Ponytail girl, you in?
Oh...

He just wants controversy but make sure to tell him our platform!
Oh, okay.

What do you say to the allegations that the recent eruption was a hoax, intended to expedite the harvest of trees from the forest?

You mean faking the volcano?

Um, did that really happen?
Allegedly, yes.
NOT YOUR LAND
Tell him our platform!

Oh, well I guess...
LIVE
6

What the...
Save the forest!!
AWOO-AWOOOO

The addition of the police pushed us over the edge. Already engulfed in confusion, the crowd broke into a full-on riot.

NOT YOUR LAND
CONDOS ARE CANCER
SAVE the OLD GROWTH
POL

Why are the police here? It's not their usual time for escort.

Do you think they're here to arrest Hedgeburn?
I should tell Thomas what's going on.

There's a ton of reporters. And cops!

What for?

I don't know. They say that Hedgeburn hired someone to fake the volcano?

CLEAR THE WAY! MOVE IT!
POLICE

The usual routine. Except I could feel that this time it wasn't usual. Something in my gut felt sour.

What's HE doing with them? Shouldn't he be in handcuffs?

CLICK.

Rex Huron, you are under arrest for con-spiracy in committing an act of terrorism.

What??
What did he do??

You have the right to remain silent.
THIS is the conspiracy! This is *@#$%&*!
CLICK

... anything you say can be held against you in a court of law...

CHAPTER EIGHT

It wasn't supposed to happen like this!

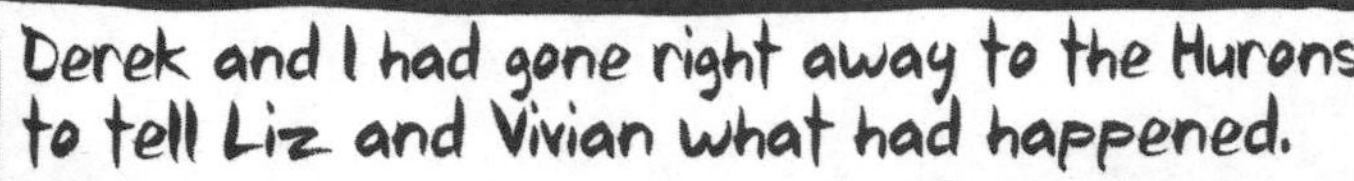
Derek and I had gone right away to the Hurons to tell Liz and Vivian what had happened.

Those cops are completely crooked. He's paying them off!

Chase said he was going to take care of it. He gave me his word!
Calm down, mom.

What are you even talking about? Dad didn't really set that explosion, did he?

He MUST be paying them off.
Mom, stop pacing and talk to me.

You know something I don't.

Your father wanted to save that forest. I was just trying to help!
What do you mean?

I have to go see Rex.
Mom, wait!

SLAM
Aghh!
She drives me crazy!

Crazy!
Uh, you wanna stay here?
Yeah, we'd better.

We went to the evening news for answers.

Tonight! Outrage by local protesters as scandal is exposed!

Picketers, already angry with the development and logging of this controversial plot of land, were uproarious today when news broke of scandal and deception.

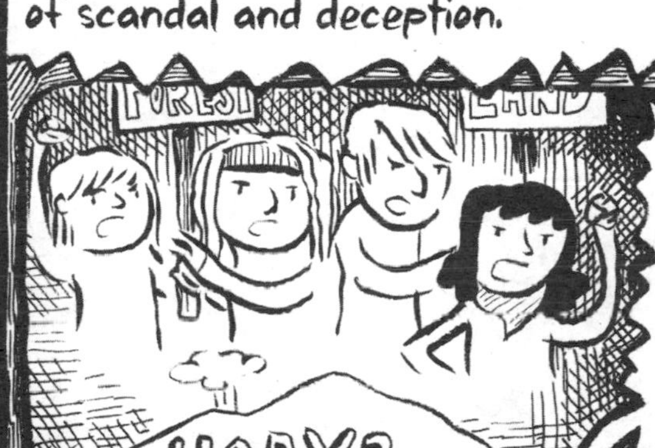
HOAX?

A memo surfaced this morning revealing that an executive at Hedgeburn Properties hired an employee to manufacture yesterday's volcanic eruption using high powered explosives.

The crime was quickly linked to one of Hedgeburn's contractors, Rex Huron, who was arrested on charges of sabotage. Chase Hedgeburn denies any involvement in this crime.

I'm appalled by this, obviously.

This kind of criminal behavior is obviously intolerable, especially from one of my own employees.

Turns out Rex has been plotting to take control the entire time he has been working for me.

Clearly this was an attempt to devalue the land and intimidate me into selling for cheap.

Perhaps the protesters have found a new enemy – one who has begun directly terrorizing the forest.
6 NEWS

This can't be true!

What was all that stuff your mom was saying about talking with Hedgeburn and him taking care of stuff?

Does she talk to him a lot?
I don't know.

I mean, I think she's met with him a few times, down in Los Angeles, like, for coffee or whatever.
CLICK

Oh yeah, coffee? Is that all they were doing?
What's that supposed to mean?

Wake up, Liz. It's pretty obvious that your mom is attracted to men with power and influence.

She's never given your dad a break since he left his other job.

She has given him every reason to act drastically.

So what are you saying? You think Rex is actually guilty?

He doesn't know what he's saying.

Liz, if you want to live in denial about it, go right ahead.

But everyone knows your mom doesn't respect him. She's all but said so herself!

If I was Rex, I'd probably blow up a mountain too!

You're just jealous because she gets to be an actress and you can't be a rock star 'cuz you're stuck with me.
Please let's not get into this.

Yeah, please let's not. No offense, but now isn't really the time to start picking apart your marriage.
Rex is in jail!

Yeah and apparently my husband thinks he deserves to be there.
I never said that.

Oh, you're right. You just said my mom is a conniving, adulterous witch.

I NEVER said that.

But that's pretty much what you were driving at, right? So what is it, Derek?

You think if their marriage is falling apart that gives you free range to give up on ours?

Come on, Liz, I have been TRYING to work on ours!

I've been trying since the day you told me you were unhappy. And I thought we were getting somewhere.

Wow, well if you call this trying, then we're in big trouble.

Apparently we are then because I don't know what else I can do.

Maybe you can go write a song about it.

After Derek left, we spent the evening waiting. What else could we do?

Vivian returned late that night, without Rex.
Hm?
CLINK

Those thugs are calling him a terrorist now!

Mom? Where have you been? Where's Dad?

He's in jail! They're keeping him without bail! They said he was a high risk of fleeing.

Can you believe that? He's never had so much as a speeding ticket!

What's going on, mom? Dad didn't really arrange that explosion, did he?
Oh Liz...

It's complicated. Things are really messed up.

Your father wanted so badly to save that forest. I was only trying to help.

He's a good man – he's good at what he does. But he could be great.

I swear I was only trying to help.
What did you do mom?
Sigh.

Your father was going to turn down the promotion. He said it went against his beliefs.

I tried to explain to him that if he had any chance of swaying Chase's policies, of saving the forest, this was it, this job.

But he wouldn't listen. So I went to Chase. We threw around the idea of a fake explosion. He said it would pressure Rex to take the job, knowing the volcano was real.

Chase went ahead with it. I don't know who he worked with, but he arranged the "eruption." But, it didn't work.

It sure looked like it worked.
Yes...

But it didn't sway Rex?
Exactly.

Rex smelled a rat, and he said he was finally going to turn Chase in.

But I knew that if Rex went after Chase, Chase would crush him. He has a lot of power.

That's how he's gotten as far as he has - he cuts down his opponents. I couldn't let Rex walk into that!

I told Chase that Rex was planning to go after him, that he had evidence to use against him.

You told him that?
Why??

I thought it would give us more leverage! I wasn't trying to threaten him. But he reacted badly.

He had Dad thrown in jail!

Sure, it was easy for him.

Everyone was already saying the volcano was a hoax, so Chase just capitalized on that. He made up that memo to frame Rex, and suddenly Chase is completely off the hook. It was so simple for him.

Even if Rex tried to use that evidence - even if he could do it from jail - no one would believe him now.

I can't believe I trusted Chase.

I can't believe you sold Dad out.

Maybe we should go see him?
...
Let's go.

This is all your fault.

COUNTY JAIL

VISITATION RULES:
DO NOT TOUCH GLASS

Are you angry?

No. It's out of my control.
229

Mom says you weren't going to accept Chase Hedgeburn's job offer.
No, I wasn't.

She said that you were going to use your evidence against him.

It was time to do the right thing.
229

Dad... you didn't have anything to do with that explosion, did you?

No.

So Hedgeburn put you here wrongfully! An investigation would prove that! You could sue him for false imprisonment! And... and... and... defamation!

She's right! When are they going to do an investigation?

I'm afraid Hedgeburn's connections here run deep. Any investigation that's happening is most likely corrupt.

He's got enough high ranking friends to keep me here until he can figure out how to keep me quiet.

What are you going to do?

I guess I'm going to wait here.

And then what?

I'm just going to wait.

You'll think of something, right?

At this point I don't think it's up to me.

Maybe it never was.

The next morning.
Morning, Bea.
Hey Sara.

Are you going to the picket line today?
No, I don't see the point. Rex isn't there anymore.

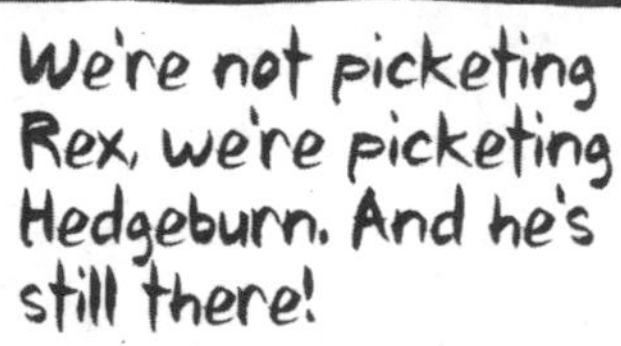
We're not picketing Rex, we're picketing Hedgeburn. And he's still there!

I just don't think I have the energy today.

Okay. See you this afternoon, then.

I worried for him.
Ding dong!

We're going to visit Dad, want to come?

Yeah.

DO NOT TOUCH GLASS
Maybe if I went to the authorities with that evidence.
No, absolutely not.

He would come after you. And like you said, no one would believe you. There's a significant conflict of interest.

You can't take the fall for something you didn't do! If you go to prison for this, Rex, I couldn't live with myself!

Viv, there are worse things than prison.

Rex...

I'm sorry that I went to him. I shouldn't have gone behind your back.
Mom?

Vivian, we don't have to talk about this with the girls here.

I thought you were making the wrong decision. I was only trying to help.

All that I ever asked was for you to trust me, Vivian!

Rex! I thought you weren't angry!

Of course I'm angry! All summer long I've been fighting this battle and I sure could have used some moral support!

I thought I was doing the right thing! I never for a second thought he would react the way he did.

You undermined my decision and you conspired with the man who would throw me in jail! You betrayed me, Vivian!

I thought it would be good to have him on our side! I thought you could win him over, and with your power, together...

Is that what you want? Do you want me to become like him?

No, Rex.

Do you want a monster for a husband?

Vivian, did you cheat with him?

Rex, the girls...

Don't try to duck out now—you opened this can of worms. Did you cheat with him?

Yes.

Good grief, Vivian! Why him?

Your director—you said he was the last one! Before that the trainer was the last!

Nothing ever changes, Vivian. How long am I supposed to put up with this?

This time was different, Rex. I did it because I love you!

That is the stupidest thing I've ever heard!

It WAS stupid, it was SO stupid. In hindsight I don't know what I was thinking. But at the time...

Listen, I ended it with him. It's over. And I hate to say it but I'm sure that has some-thing to do with why you're here in jail.

I understand if you never trust me again. But I still love you.

All I can do is beg for forgiveness.

You don't have to beg, Vivian. I love you.

I forgive you.

But it IS going to take a lot to earn back my trust.

I'll do whatever it takes, Rex.

Well, for now let's all just try to –
RUMBLE
RUMBLE

RUMBLE
Mom?

RATTLE
Rex?
RATTLE
RATTLE

Folks, visiting hour's over. We gotta move!
What's going on?

It's erupted!
DO NOT TO

This one is for real! Folks, we need to evacuate immediately!
What?
Not without my husband!
DO NOT TOUC
We're going to move your husband to another –
RUMBLE!
You get us ALL out of here right now!
Request permission to transport inmate 229.
Permission? His life is at stake – let him out!
Look, there's a squad car out front, but I'll need to cuff you between here and there.
CLINK
He's not some common criminal!
Do you think he's going to run or something?
I'm just following our emergency protocol!
Look, you can read us the safety manual in the car. Can we just get out of here??

POLICE
COUN
JAIL

Where are you taking him?
COUN
JAIL

We're evacuating all inmates to a detention facility outside of the danger radius.

Well, where is that?

Girls, go with your mom. Vivian, I love you. There's nothing you could do to lose that! When you go, take my car, okay?

You guys follow the police caravan and don't stop for anything!
Where the hell are you taking him?

We're receiving our instructions as we go, ma'am. The final destination hasn't been determined.

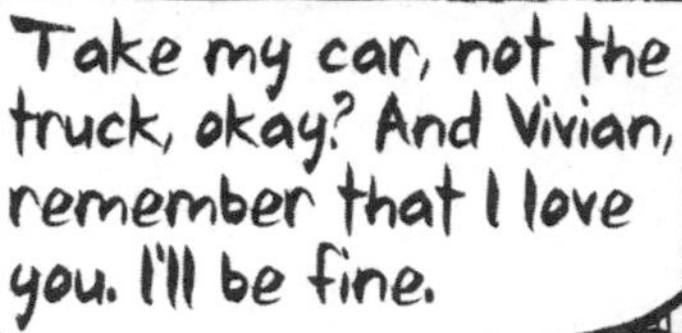
Take my car, not the truck, okay? And Vivian, remember that I love you. I'll be fine.

What about the lawn crew?

DEREK!

It's okay, Liz. We had very specific evacuation plans laid out. I'm sure Derek is safe.

We have to go get him!
You need to get to safey, Liz.

Can we ride along with my husband, please?
I'm truly sorry, ma'am.

We can only transport inmates. If you need a ride, there are civilian evacuation buses.
Rex!
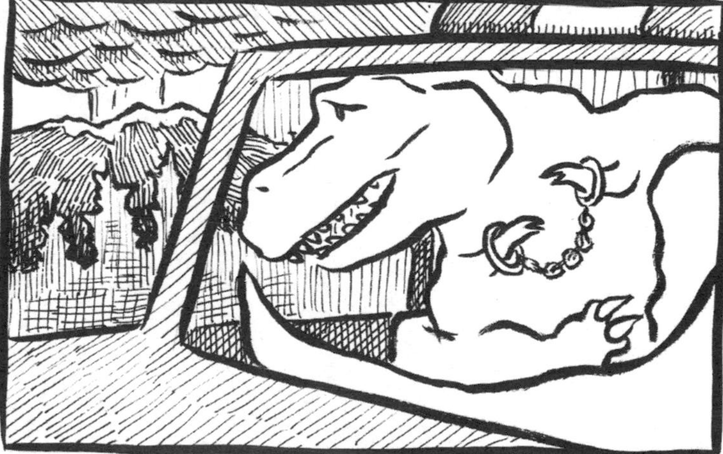

CHAPTER NINE

We followed the police to Abrams, a town sixty miles away.
WELCOME INN
SUNSET PLAZA

Like all the other inmates, they put Rex under house arrest in one of the hotel rooms and restricted him from having visitors.

314
316
318
320

At least we knew he was safe from the volcano.

We worried for those we hadn't heard from yet: Derek, Thomas, Sara. Had they gotten away before the destruction reached them?

It had happened so fast. The news reporters had already announced there were casualties.

6
BREAKING NEW
16 DEAD FROM ERUPT

Why don't you check the registry of evacuees again, dear?

We've checked it seventy times in the past three days!

And no record of the lawn crew?

No. No record of my friends from the picket line, either.

They could have been sent to another location. The whole evacuation process was a mess.

They could have been sent to another town completely!

Maybe he'll call.

But the blast had taken out cell phone towers, and communication by landlines, though possible, only worked if you knew where the other person was.

It's not right they won't let us visit your father! Don't inmates have the right to see visitors?

Well, they have the right to a phone call?
It's just not right. And anyway, what charges are they holding him on anymore?
For all they know that first explosion was just as real as the rest of the eruption!
You're right, that should clear his name, don't you think?
Liz, are you sure you don't want to check the registry again?
Sigh.
I'll go with you.
LOBBY

CAFE
REGISTRY OF EVACUATED PERSONS
FEDERAL DISASTER RELIEF
MISSING PETS! HUMANE SOCIETY
POOL
LOBBY

I need to call my son!
I'm sorry ma'am, all our lines are in use.

OF EVACUATED
He's not in here.
Neither is Thomas.

I can't believe how many people are here!
I'm feeling claustrophobic.
Let's get some fresh air.

RELIEF
GRIEF counseling Available
FREE WATER

This is so weird.
COMFORT FO

Oh my gosh.

Look at the bass player.
What?

No way.

I cannot believe that man.
Derek!
Don't wave.

Derek!
Bea, quit it!

Liz!

Liz wait!

Liz, you're okay!
I've been driving from town to town trying to find you!

And yet here you are, playing a rock show. Yeah, Derek, you look like you're real concerned.

Well come on, Liz, I've been driving for hundreds of miles in the past three days.

I've been sick at the thought of losing you. I haven't slept!

So I get here and these guys asked me to play with them, and it was something to do.
Some thing to take my mind off things.

To help take these people's minds off this disaster.

I was looking all over for you. Weren't you even looking for me?
Of course!

I've been sick over it too, Derek. I've been practically camped in front of the displaced persons' registry.

Why aren't you on there, anyway?
I didn't know about any registry.
Derek!

Well I'm sorry! This is the first volcano I've ever been caught up in!

Well, how were you looking for me, then? Knocking on individual hotel room doors?

Howdja think I hooked up with this band?

I'm so glad you're safe!

It's good to see you too, Bea.
You too.
Have you seen Thomas?

I haven't. We all got separated after the blast. I'm sure he's ok though. He's a tough kid, you know?

Where are your parents?
They put Dad under house arrest here.

They won't let us see him. Mom and Bea and I have a room on another floor. She's there right now.

Derek, you were right about Mom.
I'm sorry, Liz.

Y'know, your parents' issues aren't our issues.
I'm sorry I've yelled at you so much.
I've been selfish.

You sounded really good up there. I forgot how much I love to hear you play.

Yeah, well, in light of the volcano, it seems pretty insignificant.
Hardly!

Like you said, you're helping people cope with the disaster!

So go on, go finish your set, you rock star!

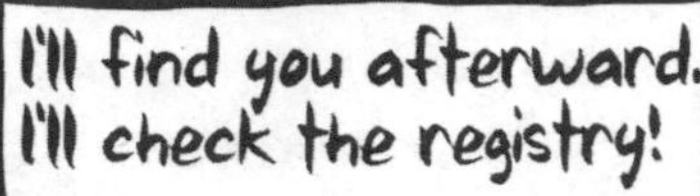
I'll find you afterward. I'll check the registry!

Smooch!

401

Mom's gone.
She left a note.

Girls,
Went to see your father. Could be late - Order a pizza!
♡ Mom
(Viv)

He can't have visitors.
Mom can only follow the rules for so long.

Later.

Later.
405

Later.
zzzz
zzzz

Then!
SLAM
Mom, what's going on? Where have you been?

Visiting your father. Didn't you see my note?
They let you in?

Hedgeburn thinks he's got the whole world wrapped around his finger with his money.

Not everyone can be bought.
The guard let you in?

Of course. He's a good man.

And it didn't hurt that I had a few extra passes to our premier.
Mom!

I needed to see your father! And it's good that I did. Apparently he keeps this...
RUSTLE RUSTLE

Is that Dad's briefcase?

...hidden in the car.

Ah, here we go.

What is that?

Anyone up for a very eventful late-night snack?

GARDEN CAFE
CAF
Please seat yourself

What are they doing here?
You get your entourage, we get ours.

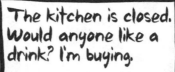

Oh, it is SO lovely to see you again, Vivian.

The kitchen is closed. Would anyone like a drink? I'm buying.
How generous.

Well, we're almost all here. I'd love to get this over with.

Who else is...

Dad!

Well isn't this nice.

Can we begin?
Yes.

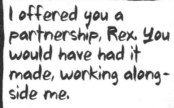

I offered you a partnership, Rex. You would have had it made, working along-side me.

And look at how you repay me.

Rumor has it you've got quite the dirt on me, but I wonder...

...what could possibly make it worth all this trouble, calling me up here from Los Angeles?

All this trouble? You had me thrown in jail, Chase!

You tore me away from my family in the middle of a natural disaster. You've destroyed my good name in this state.

You've given me every incentive in the world to turn you in as the crook that you are.

Yes, I know. So here's where I make an offer.

The deal is, you're released from jail, you keep your mouth shut, and I sell you the land for almost nothing.

It's like none of this ever happened and you get that precious little plot of charred, stupid forest. What a souvenir!

We're not interested.

You wanted to save that forest, well here's your chance, Rex. It can be a moral victory for you.

Look, I'm prepared to strike a very generous deal if it means sweeping this whole thing under the rug.

I don't think you quite grasp the reality of your situation, Chase. You're in no position to make a deal.

You can't sell that land, because it was never yours. Your father promised it to the people.

And you know as well as everyone else how that played out in court.

And I also know WHY it played out that way.

Oh right, your little "evidence." My guess is you're bluffing. You don't have a thing.

Viv?
Chase, you might recall this email which you sent a few months ago.
Ahem.

"Rex, picketers getting to be a nuisance? If you need any muscle, I have friends in the police force who would be glad to rough them up a bit."

Another one: "Rex, the environmental lobbyists gearing to appeal court ruling. No need to worry, though, Judge K is only a dollar sign away."

Isn't she dramatic? We'll have an Oscar on the mantle before we know it.

Those emails don't prove a thing.

Did you think that's all we have? Those emails are just the beginning, Chase. I've got a brief-case full of "dirt."

See, you've been so arrogant thinking that you're above the law that you've gotten sloppy in your business and sloppy in your crimes.

You've left quite a trail, to tell you the truth.

Are you trying to blackmail me?

I wouldn't give you the luxury of being black-mailed, Chase. And I wouldn't deprive the people of justice.

What do you want from me? I've already offered to sell you the land for pennies. You could give it back to the public - wasn't that your goal all along?

You'd sell it for pennies now, because you think it's lost its value. But that land is priceless. That volcano barely touched it - you were the one to desecrate it.

You've go to prison for a few years. You'll lose business, you'll lose some of your investors.

It could be much worse for you, if I pressed charges for false imprisonment.

If I turned over the evidence for each of your crooked deals, every bribe your hand has signed off on.

But I won't. And in exchange, you'll turn yourself in for bribing a state judge.

I offered you a full partnership, Rex. Look at you, you're a lawn mower. You could have been as powerful as I am.

He's more powerful than you are.

I'd keep a close eye on your wife, Rex. She WILL cheat again.

Frankly, your opinion does not concern me in the least.

I tried to give you a chance, Chase. You should be grateful you're getting off this easy.

I doubt he could have planned it from the beginning, but the way Rex maneuvered the negotiations it seemed as if he had been working out the details since day one. Maybe, somehow, he had.

Hedgeburn turned himself in to the authorities and cooperated during the investigation.

Rex, in exchange, kept his word and didn't sue Hedgeburn for planting evidence and having him falsely charged. Chase would go to prison anyway.

Rex was vindicated and his charges dropped when authorities realized he had not set the first explosion.

LOBBY

This was confirmed by a signed confession, sent in by one of Rex's employees.

Uff.
Oh, sorry.

Thomas!
Bea, hi!

What happened to you?

Oh, heh, I kind of got caught up in the eruption. Crazy huh?

What? Are you okay? How did that happen?

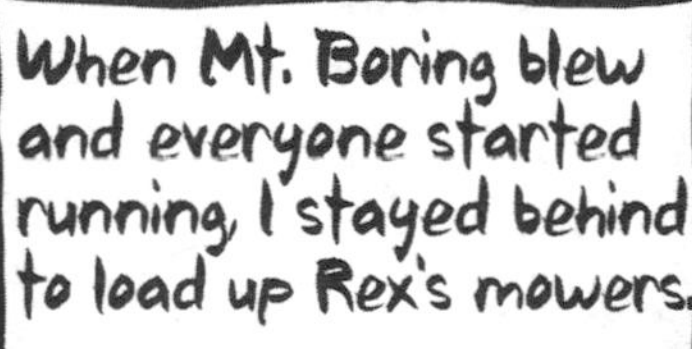
When Mt. Boring blew and everyone started running, I stayed behind to load up Rex's mowers.

Are you stupid? You could have been killed!
If only.

Thomas...
No, really. I owed to to Rex after what I did.
What...

I set that first explosion, Bea. Hedgeburn paid me to do it.
What? Why?

I had nothing else going for me. You were gone. The job was gonna end soon. And money talks.

You turned yourself in. The signed confession, it was yours.

I thought I would try to make things right. Rex never belonged in prison—I did.

But you're not... the cops didn't arrest you.

Nope. How's this for irony: the volcano wiped out any case the authorities might have had against ANYone.

I can't even manage to get myself properly arrested!

Hey listen, I'm going to be leaving town for a while.

Oh, um, you are? Where are you going?

I dunno. Chicago maybe? Somewhere without any volcanos, haha.

I know you can't come with me, but maybe we could write?
Yeah, of course.

Unless, maybe, you could come? I mean, are you still tring to figure stuff out? Find your place?

Um, I don't know, Thomas. I think I may have found it. At least for now.

Don't sound so sad to say it.

You've been staring at the ground for so long. It's time to enjoy the view.

Hey, I'm sorry I haven't been more honest with you about things.

Let's stay in touch, okay?
Yeah, let's.

LOBBY
I'll miss you.

He wasn't beyond saving but we both knew it wasn't my job to save him.

What could I save him from? He had survived the volcano — surely something, or someone, had a hand in that.

Maybe the ravaging molten rock was the very thing that would warm him where he had become so cold.

It took a few days for the ash to settle on Mt. Boring. As for the further reaching implications, that took much longer to sort out.

After Hedgeburn turned himself in, the court ruling in his favor was thrown out and the elder Hedgeburn's will was finally honored.

The land was inherited by the people of California and would eventually be transformed into a state park.

FUTURE SITE
OF YOUR NEW
CALIFORNIA
STATE PARK

"Eventually," because the damage caused by the volcano was catastrophic.
It would take months to clean all of the debris.
SAVE THE FOREST
It would take years before the first signs of new life would appear.
But they would surely appear.
In the weeks after the eruption, Rex ran uncontested for chair of the forest restoration committee. This would eventually meld into a permanent position as Park Ranger.
Behind us you'll see the formidable volcano, Mount Elizabeth.
Would you kids believe I was sitting in a jail cell when this beauty erupted?
Cool!
CLICK!

On the front end of the restoration project, Rex recruited a number of regulars from the picket line, including my friends James and Emily, and my housemate Sara, who had all survived the eruption with stories to tell.

Rex offered me a similar job, which I accepted only after weighing it at length with another offer: a position with a little lawn care company called Huron and Copperman...

Mowing lawn by day...

Glen, Larry, load up the mowers for the Vansen Park job!
I'm calling to confirm our bid on your landscaping project...

...and rocking out by night.

LAVA
MAGMA

Vivian continued to pursue her acting career, but stuck to roles with the local theater.

I won't pretend to know the details of their personal life. No one is perfect, but I think Vivian was trying her best.

And I believe Rex loved her more than ever.

Amidst all of the destruction from the volcano, 5% of the old growth had been spared. By some miracle it wasn't touched. This was where I liked to go to write my letters to Thomas.

Letters which I would never send, since I had no idea where he ended up.

Somehow, though, I knew he was okay.

His parting encouragement reminded me to be happy for the peace I'd found.

And so one day...

Inspired by nothing besides that peace and fading restlessness...

I decided to stop writing him...

...and just enjoy the view.

ACKNOWLEDGEMENTS

My most humble and heartfelt thanks to the following people, without whom this book simply would not exist.

The Xeric Foundation, for your generous financial contribution which made publishing possible.

Mom and Dad, for your endless encouragement and sincere interest. Your belief emboldened me to make this book a reality. Meagan, Shawn, and Rod, for creating and taking risks, and so inspiring me to do the same. Grandma Bordeleau, for your friendship and support while I find my way in this life, as an artist and beyond. Zech Bard, for your passionate belief in my story, and the countless hours you worked to make sure it saw the light of day. You are truly amazing. Olga Lukomsky, for all of your excellent assistance and dedication to this project. Jen Clemens, for giving me a home, a studio, and a playground all under one roof. Fun is the best! Todd Fadel, for your contagious energy that enlivened me, and your community spirit that connected me. Laura Cone, for introducing me to the zine-scene and always cheering on your friends (I'm glad to be one of them). Holly Trasti, for fanning the little rock-and-roll/comics flame that began in high school. Nate Grubbs, for the custom "GN" font, the beautiful video, and lots of inspiring art theorizing. Rachael Kerns, for your expert reassurance through this process, your enthusiasm for my passion, and for so much material for future stories.

Thank you to my initial draft readers: Alex, Anthony, Arek, Dana, Dharma, Diane, Len, Rachel, Emily, Gary, Gwen, Holly, Jeannie, Kyle, Laura, Meagan, Molly, Robert, Sean, and Shawn.
Thank you to my friends who helped with various tasks along the way (long live the erasing parties!), Abbi, Arek, Aron, Beth, Crystal, Darren, Gene, Jamie, Lauren, Liz, Kim, Nick, Seth, and the IPRC.
Thank you to the amazing musicians who contributed to the soundtrack: Abbi & Issaac, Agents of Future, Andrea Carter, Andrew Holzem, Bognor, Bruhn, Fishboy, Girls Doing Embroidery, Great Wilderness, Holly & the Nice Lions, Jonathan Atchley, Lofty Toms, No Kind of Rider, Recreation Station, RED on RED!, Team Fadel, and Upsidedown Cat.

Finally, thank you Jesus, for all of the above, and everything else.

Breena Wiederhoeft grew up in northern Wisconsin where she learned she had this thing called an imagination. She started drawing comics at a young age, and eventually began a diary-style webcomic called Easel Ain't Easy. When not drawing or writing comics, Breena can be found playing music, taking naps, and visiting with the neighborhood cats. *Picket Line* is her first graphic novel, and the winner of a Xeric Award. Breena currently lives in Portland, Oregon, where she is working on her second graphic novel.

Look for Breena's next graphic novel, *Oaks*, coming 2012.

www.easelainteasy.com